History of Virginia

A Captivating Guide to the History of the Mother of States, Starting from Jamestown through the American Revolution and the Battle of Spotsylvania Court House to the Present

Free Bonus from Captivating History
(Available for a Limited time)

Hi History Lovers!

Now you have a chance to join our exclusive history list so you can get your first history ebook for free as well as discounts and a potential to get more history books for free! Simply visit the link below to join.

Captivatinghistory.com/ebook

Also, make sure to follow us on Facebook, Twitter and Youtube by searching for Captivating History.

Contents

Introduction

Virginia, known as the mother of states and the mother of presidents, has had a rich heritage and culture that began well before its admission as a state on June 25, 1788. Like most other states in America, Virginia's history dates back tens of thousands of years ago when the continent's first people arrived by crossing the Bering Strait via a land bridge that was once located between Russia and Alaska. Although the state today is home to less than 30,000 Native Americans, it was once home to tens of thousands more. Over thousands of years, the native tribes developed from nomadic hunter-gatherer tribes into more sedentary communities with complicated political, spiritual, economic, and social systems and traditions. Since Virginia's landscape is so varied, the first people's habits, culture, and beliefs really depended on their location. For example, those in forests had access to different building materials and flora and fauna than those in the valleys, who had access to more rich and fertile soil. Although Virginia is the home of the United States' most well-known (though not entirely accurate) Native American story, that of Pocahontas, little is actually known about the Virginian tribes which inhabited the land until the days of colonization. Even then, much of their culture was stripped by missionaries, making it impossible to know the depth of their early history.

Over the course of the 15th, 16th, and 17th centuries, European forces were avidly attempting to colonize America. However, while South America was being explored, the United States would have many failed settlements until, finally, in 1607, the British would create the first successful settlement in the US, located in Jamestown, Virginia. While the colonizers and Native American population would have many altercations, most of which were devastating to the Native American tribes whose presence preceded that of the Europeans by thousands of years, the two groups would also experience more breakthroughs and periods of peace than in other colonies in America. The colony of Virginia would remain under British rule for around a century and a half, yet, during that time, Virginia was developing its own unique and rich culture, as was the case in the other nearby British colonies. The Virginia colony's original culture mainly revolved around tobacco farming, which would help to form the colony's economy, wealthy families, political system, and ideologies.

Throughout Virginia's development, settlers began to grow tired of the British government, which continued to oppressively control their political system, economy, taxes, religion, and infrastructures. Before long, public dissatisfaction would culminate in the American Revolutionary War. Joining forces with the other thirteen British colonies, which had come to the same conclusions, Virginia fought what seemed at the time an impossible battle. It succeeded in gaining independence from England, acquiring early statehood in the newly formed United States of America. Virginians would play an important role in the forming of America, and many even consider three Virginians—Patrick Henry, Thomas Jefferson, and George Washington—to be the voice, pen, and sword of the American Revolution.

Virginia would suffer greatly in the post-revolutionary period, as extensive tobacco farming had depleted the nutrients in the soil. As tobacco had been the crux of Virginia's economy, the state was forced to reestablish itself entirely. The tobacco farmers who had employed slaves to work on their plantations began selling laborers at an incredible rate, quickly transforming Richmond, Virginia's capital city, into one of the largest slave markets in the world. Meanwhile, as Virginia's economy suffered, Virginians migrated in search of economic opportunities elsewhere, spreading their ideologies and systems to newly-forming states, mainly in the South.

Since the origination of the tobacco crop, Virginia's tobacco farmers had used slave labor to help on their plantations. From the very beginning, slaves were seen as a tool for growing wealth and a display of one's fortunes, so it is no surprise that owning slaves was completely intertwined with Virginia's culture. So, when it came time to pick sides in the American Civil War, Virginia became a leading force for the Confederates—the Confederate capital was even moved to Richmond. Virginia would host more Civil War battlefields than any other state in America and produce some of the most influential military strategists, notably Robert E. Lee and Stonewall Jackson. Yet the state would find itself on the losing side of the Civil War and worse off than many of the other Confederate states. Virginia would become so divided during this conflict that one-third of its land would split off and form a new state known as West Virginia.

Just as in the post-Revolutionary War years, Virginia was forced to completely rebuild itself in the post-Civil War years, which it would successfully do, returning to many of its old systems and ideologies, much to the dismay of Virginia's African American population. Still, the state would continue to evolve, and following the First World War, Virginia would begin to invest much of its money into military purposes. By the Second World War, the state would become known as America's military hub, housing both the country's CIA headquarters and the Pentagon. Today, Virginia has redeveloped an incredibly successful economy yet remains a somewhat divided state. For many years, it was even considered a swing state (although now it is more Democratic than Republican), and the political and social roller coaster leading to this point is complex and extremely interesting.

Chapter 1 – Virginia's Early History (Beginning of Virginia's History–1607)

Virginia's First People

Long before Jamestown, Virginia, became the home of the first European settlement in the United States of America, the region of Virginia was inhabited by a group of migrant hunters known as the Paleo-Indians. These first people of Virginia were believed to be natives of Asia who, while hunting and pursuing prehistoric mammals, traveled along a former land bridge across the Bering Strait. Although the first people's route to the Americas was certainly far from easy, it was not as difficult as it may seem to us today. The shortest distance between Russia and Alaska is just under ninety kilometers, and the region of Beringia is believed to have been abundant in both edible plants and huntable prey, which sustained the travelers throughout their long journey. Many millennia ago, all of Canada and some of the United States were covered by massive glaciers. However, over thousands of years, the large glaciers melted, causing the sea levels to rise by a few hundred feet and leaving no trace of the Bering land bridge. Despite the fact that the Bering land bridge has been flooded for potentially 10,000 years, historians believe that the region of Beringia would have resembled a tundra, similar to those in modern-day Canada, Alaska, and Siberia.

There is actually much contention among historians, archeologists, paleontologists, and scientists as to the exact time America's first people arrived. The most common opinion is that the first people of America arrived sometime between 10,000 and 12,000 years ago. However, the famous Cactus Hill archaeological site, which is located only about fifty miles from Virginia's capital city of Richmond, proves otherwise. The Cactus Hill site was discovered in the 1990s and is believed to be one of the—if not the—oldest archaeological sites in both Virginia and the United States, as it is dated to around 18,000 to 20,000 years ago. Although other archaeological sites have been found that predate Cactus Hill by 100,000 years in some cases, there is not yet enough evidence at these sites to prove they are as old as they seem. Regardless, the evidence of prehistoric occupation at Cactus Hill has caused historians to reexamine not only the first settlers' date of arrival but also their route and method of arrival. Since the discovery of Cactus Hill, historians have questioned why the first settlers, who are believed to have come from Alaska, would have first settled on the eastern coast of America in Virginia rather than the western coast or even Central America. This would suggest that either the first people of America arrived via the Atlantic Ocean from Europe or Cactus Hill is, in fact, nowhere near the first native settlement in America, and the first people arrived long before 20,000 years ago. The latter explanation is more likely and commonly believed.

Regardless of exactly when the first people in America arrived, there is much more known and little contention about the lifestyle of these early inhabitants. From archeological discoveries made at the Cactus Hill site, as well as other sites throughout Virginia, historians have discovered that the first inhabitants of Virginia were likely part of the Clovis culture. They were named for the weapons they used, known as Clovis points, recognizable by their fluted, almost surfboard-like shape. The first people of Virginia are said to have been nomadic hunter-gatherers who used Clovis point weapons to hunt, carve, and cut up deer, rabbit, bison, and other Virginian prey. Since the region of Virginia has various landscapes and terrains, separate bands developed their own diets, lifestyles, and culture depending on the region in which they lived. The first people in the Appalachian region of Virginia, migrating through the tundra-like mountains, of course lived completely differently than those in the grasslands and forests of the Shenandoah Valley and the northern region of the state. Until around 10, 000 years ago when the glaciers located throughout Canada finally melted, the Virginian climate was tens of degrees colder than it is today, and the harsh conditions forced the bands of people to migrate, seeking areas to camp every season that would not only have an abundance of food but also offer protection from the winds and cold in the winter and the roaming animals and hot sun in the summer.

Archaic Period

Over the course of the years the first people inhabited Virginia, the temperatures warmed up. Eventually, migrating no longer became a necessity, allowing the previously nomadic bands to establish tribes and settlements. Since rising temperatures caused the glaciers to the north to melt, many of the areas in Virginia that had previously been inhabited by the first people were flooded, which not only changed the landscape of the region but also altered the fertility of the soil and the accessibility of flora and fauna. By around 6000 BCE, the lifestyles of many of the first settlers had completely changed as a result of the rising temperatures, making it difficult to truly understand how the first people of Virginia lived. Our only information is based on archeological sites and the habits of the Native Americans, who are descendants of the first people.

From 6000 BCE to 2500 BCE, known as the Middle Archaic period, the first people developed many new tools and weapons, including spears, hooks, axes, mortars, and pestles. With more efficient tools, the natives were able to cut down trees more efficiently, which not only allowed them to build more permanent settlements but also promoted the growth of fruit, nut and legume shrubs, trees, and plants that required more sunlight to grow. With less harsh weather conditions and more stability in their lifestyle, the native population of Virginia continued to grow, slowly exploring just about every area in the region. The various tribes continued to establish small villages, now equipped with soapstone cooking vessels, ceramic pots, gardens, and various other tools that made a more sedentary life possible. It was not uncommon for people of various tribes to marry, which would often combine both tribes and merge their cultures and lifestyles. By the year 1000 BCE, the hundreds of small tribes that had inhabited the region of Virginia had culminated into three main cultural groups known as the Algonquian, Iroquoian, and Siouan.

The Algonquian, who inhabited various regions of Virginia, were both nomadic and sedentary, known for their extensive villages and their hunting and gathering migratory lifestyles. To travel efficiently, the Algonquian constructed easy-to-carry boats, mostly canoes, which allowed them to visit various villages and make contact and trade with other tribes and cultural groups. The Iroquois lived along the river banks and valleys and led completely sedentary lives, which allowed them to establish villages with many large homes, complete gardens, tools, crafts, and more. Similar to the Algonquian, the Iroquois were known to construct canoes, which they used to fish, hunt prey, and explore the region for trading sites and materials. Very little is known of the final Virginian tribal linguistic group, the Siouan, as they rarely interacted with Europeans. What we do know about the Siouan tribes is that they rarely used waterways, especially compared to the Algonquian and Iroquois tribes, which meant that the Siouan's travel was limited and they ate much less fish than the former tribes.

Woodland Period

The period from around 1200 BCE to the arrival of the colonists is viewed as the Native Americans' Woodland period, during which time most of the tribes had established complex societies with impressively intricate housing and political, trade, religious, and social systems in place. By the 17th century, tribes had established either semi-permanent or permanent villages, often with hierarchical leaders who would help forge both political and trade alliances among various other tribes—even those from the other cultural groups. Most tribes had some form of advanced agriculture. For example, many farmed efficiently using the symbiotic relationship between corn, squash, and beans, which later became known as the "sister crops" or the "three sisters" since the crops grow best when planted near each other. Techniques such as this, along with knowing what foods grew best, when they should be planted and harvested, and how to take care of them, were all discovered through years of experimentation—laboring on the land and planting various crops. Archeological sites from the Woodland period reveal that the tribes had religious traditions and/or rituals, the most notable of which was their burial rituals. Those who had deceased would be buried in a large mound among items they cherished and ones that would be of use in the afterworld.

Despite the lack of information truly known about the natives who inhabited Virginia during this time period, we do understand that they had by this point—and certainly by the arrival of the Europeans—developed complex societies and cultures. For the most part, the state was split as such: the Algonquian tribes were located along the Atlantic Coast, the Iroquois were scattered south of Virginia's tidewater region, and the Siouan were mostly established in higher elevations above the fall line. There were, of course, many alliances and chiefdoms among the tribes, notably the Iroquois and Siouan alliance. However, the most powerful chiefdom of them all was by far the Powhatan Paramount Chiefdom, featured in the film *Pocahontas*. Its main character, Pocahontas, was inspired by the real daughter of the Great Powhatan.

Although the exact date of the formation of the chiefdom is not known, it is believed the Powhatan Paramount Chiefdom could be, at most, 700 years old. The Powhatan Paramount Chiefdom (also known as Tsenacomoco) was said to include somewhere around thirty different Algonquian tribes, which inhabited present-day Jamestown and the surrounding coastal region. Each tribe had its own hierarchy and leader but was ultimately led by the head of the Powhatan Paramount Chiefdom, known simply as the Powhatan. The Powhatan Paramount Chiefdom was in some ways the first city in the United States, as the word "Tsenacommacah" is said to translate to "densely inhabited land." This makes sense, as by the mid-17th century, there are estimated to have been somewhere around 15,000 Native Americans in the Powhatan Paramount Chiefdom. This means that the Powhatan Paramount Chiefdom would have represented almost a third of the Native Americans inhabiting Virginia at the time. By the arrival of the Europeans in 1607, there was believed to have been approximately 50,000 Native Americans in the region of Virginia, although this is hardly an accurate or exact claim by any means. Despite the speed at which the Powhatan Paramount Chiefdom had grown both in population and land area, everything would change for the Tsenacomoco and the Native American people, in general, in 1607 when the first Europeans arrived and established their first settlement in present-day Jamestown, Virginia—right in the heart of the Powhatan Paramount Chiefdom territory.

Chapter 2 – Discovery and First Explorations and Settlements in America (1000–1607)

Viking Settlements in America

Meanwhile, as the Native American population in Virginia spread, developed, and grew, the Europeans were beginning to explore and colonize the globe, with the eastern coast of the United States soon to come. Although Christopher Columbus is celebrated and remembered as the first European to discover America, this is factually incorrect. Furthermore, Columbus was late by close to 500 years. The earliest European exploration in the Americas was not that of the Spanish, but the Vikings, whose exact reasons for explorations remain mostly unknown. However, some historians say that the Vikings' discovery and later settlement in America were accidental, as their boat was blown off course to Greenland. Others maintain they were in search of riches while, while still others believe the Vikings were in search of new land, as their home had become overpopulated.

Whatever the reason, the first Viking expedition, led by Icelandic explorer Leif Erikson, was said to have landed in North America sometime just after the year 1000. Leif Erikson and his crew disembarked on Canada's eastern coast in the present-day Canadian province of Newfoundland and Labrador, quickly building small Viking-style homes with local timber; the roofs were covered in sod. Although subsequent expeditions helped populate the Viking settlement, the Vikings did not stay long in Canada or have a chance to explore the rest of the Americas due to their poor relations with the Native Americans. It is believed that tensions developed after the Vikings killed some Native Americans who fell asleep in the Viking camp. Since the Vikings did not remain in America and their explorations did not inspire other countries to immediately travel to America, they are often not credited with the discovery of the "New World." This title is instead given to the Spanish explorer Christopher Columbus.

Christopher Columbus

In 1492, nearly half a millennium after the Vikings first set foot in Canada, Christopher Columbus—after thirty-six days of sailing—debarked in the present-day Bahamas, which he immediately claimed for Spain. Over the next decade, Christopher Columbus would lead three more voyages to the Western Hemisphere, landing in Cuba, Santo Domingo, and Jamaica, all three of which he claimed for Spain. He also briefly debarked in other Central and South American countries. Although on his second trip to America he landed in Puerto Rico and claimed it for Spain, Christopher Columbus never did set foot in the mainland of the United States, and neither did any other European until the 16th century.

Other Explorations

Throughout the end of the 15th century and start of the 16th century, the future United States remained totally untouched by the Europeans, even as John Cabot and Hernán Cortés were respectively exploring Eastern Canada and Mexico. However, the territory of the United States would not be ignored by the Europeans for long. Over the next few decades, various explorers would travel through parts of the United States, and many would attempt to establish settlements—all of which failed until Jamestown in the 17th century.

The most notable of these explorations and settlements was San Miguel de Gualdape in South Carolina, led by Spanish explorer Lucas Vázquez de Ayllón in 1526, making it the first official European settlement in the United States. Although San Miguel de Gualdape was established by the Spanish eighty-one years before the English would settle in Jamestown, Virginia, most do not consider it to be the first United States settlement since the entire population either died from illnesses or abandoned the settlement within a few months.

Another notable, early, failed United States settlement was Roanoke in North Carolina, which the English failed to populate two times. This settlement is well known due to the fact that John White, the founder of the second Roanoke settlement, traveled back to England after founding the settlement. Upon his return to Roanoke, he found that the entire settlement, along with members of his own family, had completely vanished, with only the word "Croatoan" carved on a tree. For many years, the Roanoke settlement was known as the "Lost Colony," and the reason for the settlement's disappearance remained a mystery. Today, archaeologists and historians credit the Roanoke settlement's disappearance to the drought which plagued the area during that time (discovered through tree-ring data) and the Croatan Native American tribe, which the Roanoke settlement may have joined or had conflict with.

The Race for the United States

Although the Spanish had success claiming Mexico, the Europeans were unable to establish a stable presence in the United States (or Canada, for that matter) until the start of the 17th century, at which point a colonization race began between France, Spain, and England. While all three countries sought trading resources and new land to colonize, England was the slowest of the three. Spain focused mostly on South America and Mexico, while France focused on the north, quickly establishing settlements in Acadia (northeastern Canada and the United States) in 1604 and Port Royal (in present-day Nova Scotia, Canada) in 1605.

How British Colonization Took Place

The turning point that changed everything for England and finally allowed British exploration to catch up to the Spanish and the French was King James I deciding to charter companies to explore America in 1606. At this point, England had chartered companies to trade in other European countries and some of Spain's America. King James I specifically instructed that the trade companies colonize "between parallels 34° and 41° north and the other anywhere between 38° and 45° north," which was, in essence, the eastern coast of the United States. The charter also granted the shareholders the right to fund and populate the land as they liked, and settlers were guaranteed the rights of English subjects. However, King James I and the British Crown would be in charge of the land's government, and it was forbidden to make laws that contradicted those in England. Two companies were quickly chartered: the Plymouth Company and the Virginia Company of London (Virginia Company), the latter of which was supported by Sir Walter Raleigh—the man who had sent John White to create the failed Roanoke settlement.

Although both the Plymouth Company and the Virginia Company would successfully reach the United States in 1607 and set up their own respective settlements in present-day Maine and Virginia, the Plymouth Company's settlement in Maine would be abandoned within the next year. On the other hand, the Virginia Company's settlement in present-day Jamestown, named for King James I, would be permanent, making Jamestown England's first successful settlement in the Americas.

The Voyage to and Arrival in Jamestown

In December of 1606, somewhere around 144 settlers set out from England upon three ships known as the *Susan Constant*, the *Godspeed*, and the *Discovery*. Although the ships were the property of the Virginia Company, few members of the Virginia Company were aboard. Rather, the Virginia Company merchants simply funded the trip by supplying the ships and hiring employees to safely bring the settlers to America in exchange for eventual repayment and a percentage of the money the settlers made from trade and resources in America. Aboard the ships were captain of the *Godspeed*, Bartholomew Gosnold, captain of the *Susan Constant* Christopher Newport, and captain of the *Discovery*, John Ratcliffe, and John Smith. It is said that all but twenty or so of the passengers arrived in the United States when the ships debarked on May 13, 1607, in what would formally become Jamestown, Virginia. Although Jamestown had humid temperatures and marshy grounds at the time of the settlers' arrival, the captains chose to land and set up their new settlement in Jamestown because it seemed unoccupied. (Although it may have been at the time, it was of course in the territory of the Powhatan Paramount Chiefdom.) Its location made it easy to defend and to bring ships close by.

Christopher Newport, part of the deciding process for the new settlement's location, was employed by the Virginia Company to lead a total of four more voyages between England and Jamestown over the next five years, each time bringing more supplies and settlers to help fortify the new British settlement. John Smith is likely the most well-remembered passenger on the first voyage due to his relations with the Virginian Native American population, which inspired the popular Disney film, *Pocahontas*. John Smith was a veteran soldier who had fought in the Dutch War of Independence and the Ottoman–Habsburg wars, and in the latter, he was promoted to the rank of captain. After leaving the army, John Smith managed to join the 100 or so Englishmen making their way to Virginia. Upon arriving in Jamestown, John Smith was admitted to the colony's governing council alongside Captain Newport, Captain Gosnold, Captain Ratcliffe, George Kendall, John Martin, and finally, Edward-Maria Wingfield, who was a major investor in the Virginia Company and would become the leader of the colony's governing council.

Chapter 3 – The First Years in Jamestown (1607–1619)

The first year in Jamestown was nowhere near easy for the settlers, who were exhausted after having just spent about five months at sea. Like many of the long expeditions across the ocean at that time, the three ships that reached Virginia were essentially breeding grounds for sicknesses, many of which developed from lack of nutrients. Upon arriving in Jamestown, the settlers had little experience with the humid temperatures and no experience with the local flora and fauna, which made it difficult to find food. Consequently, many more settlers died from illnesses and starvation. The only likely reason the settlement survived was John Smith, who quickly explored the region, drew up maps, found food sources, and—most notably—forged relations with the local Native American population.

Relationship with the Powhatan Paramount Chiefdom

What the settlers had believed to be unoccupied land had, of course, been occupied not only by Native Americans but by the most powerful chiefdom in Virginia: the Algonquians of the Powhatan Paramount Chiefdom. By 1607, the Powhatan Paramount Chiefdom had grown into a flourishing community that inhabited most of Virginia's eastern coast. The English would have had little luck finding unoccupied land no matter where they had tried to settle. Since both the Native Americans and the new British settlers were in constant need of more farmable land and huntable game, conflicts between the two groups began almost immediately upon the latter's arrival.

Warring between the two groups began, although casualties were quite small at first. Both sides were in many ways equally matched: the Native Americans in numbers and experience in the land and the English with immunities against illnesses they brought to America and more advanced weaponry. The tensions grew and culminated in December of 1607 when John Smith and a group of men were exploring the Chickahominy River, which flows through Virginia from the James River only a few miles from the Jamestown Settlement. The group was ambushed by Native Americans from the Powhatan Paramount Chiefdom, and John was promptly brought before Chief Powhatan. As the two groups were at war, John Smith was sentenced to death. However, just before Chief Powhatan's ruling was about to be carried out, John Smith was saved by ten-year-old Matoaka, daughter of Chief Powhatan, who situated herself between the condemned and his executioners—except, when Matoaka introduced herself to the English, she instead used a nickname: Pocahontas. Both John Smith himself and historians of today question(ed) whether the young Pocahontas truly stood up for him, risking her reputation and quite possibly her life, or if her father instructed her to do so as a ceremonial act of sorts to induct the British as allies.

Over the next few months, the Native Americans helped teach the settlers how to survive in the Virginian landscape. To smooth over relations, the two groups exchanged a young man each. The Native Americans sent over Namontack to teach the settlers how to acquire sustenance, and the English sent a thirteen-year-old named Thomas Savage, who would learn the Algonquin customs and language with the aid of Pocahontas. Having been the man who kept the peace between the Native Americans and the British, John Smith was elected president of the Jamestown settlement on September 10,

1608. He quickly changed the settlers' lives, requiring more disciplined work from the colonists.

However, despite the settlers' hard work to develop their town and acquire sustenance, the colonists could not fulfill their own food requirements, mostly due to the horrendously record-breaking drought that plagued the region that year. John Smith and the Jamestown settlement began depending almost entirely on the Powhatan Paramount Chiefdom for food, which caused a strain on their relationship and drained the Native Americans of their own respective food supply. By 1609, the Powhatan Paramount Chiefdom was tired of feeding the settlers, and Chief Powhatan planned to attack and kill John Smith and his fellow Englishmen. However, the chiefdom's element of surprise was spoiled by Chief Powhatan's daughter Pocahontas, who sneaked through the woods in the dead of night to warn John Smith of her father's plan. Once again, it is not exactly known whether she acted alone or whether there was once again some greater plan at play.

Despite the serious threats on the settlers' lives due to lack of food and rising tensions with the Native Americans, the groups would experience essentially no deaths during this period. And, as a group of women had arrived on one of Newport's voyages the previous year, the settlers' population would grow due to incoming settlers and new births. The only immediate effects of Pocahontas' warnings to John Smith were that she stopped visiting the Jamestown colony and the settlers stopped requesting as much food from the Native Americans. This leads many to believe Pocahontas was sent to warn John Smith strategically so that the Powhatan Paramount Chiefdom could stop supplying the settlers' food without negatively affecting their relationship.

Before long, the Powhatan Paramount Chiefdom moved its capital to Orapax, further away from the Jamestown settlement. Despite the distanced connection between the two groups, they stayed on relatively good terms over the next year. The Englishmen even sent another young boy, fourteen-year-old Henry Spelman, to join Thomas Savage among the Powhatan Chiefdom. However, even the strained relationship the two groups had at this point did not last long. Within the year, Henry Spelman decided to leave the Powhatan Chiefdom and join another Native American tribe, the Potomac. This was, in many ways, an act of betrayal to the Powhatan Chiefdom. Although young Henry Spelman was sentenced to death, Pocahontas would once again stand against her father and the Powhatan Chiefdom to save the Englishman's life. Regardless of whether Henry Spelman was killed, the relationship between the settlers and the Powhatan Paramount Chiefdom had soured, and Thomas Savage was promptly sent back to the Jamestown settlement, ending the period of amity between the two groups.

Although the settlers had been lacking in food, Jamestown had been developing remarkably under John Smith's leadership. There were close to no deaths under his charge, and the settlers managed to dig a successful well, build more houses and forts, plant crops and make tar, pitch, and soap ash, and overall fortify Jamestown. However, things were about to change for the town of Jamestown — not due to the Native Americans nearby, but to new orders from England.

On May 23, 1609, the Virginia Company, most of whom were living in London, received a charter from the king demanding that the president of Jamestown (who at this time was John Smith) be replaced with a council led by a governor, whom the Virginia Company was to choose. The Virginia Company chose Sir Thomas Gates to lead the Jamestown colony for one year as the settlement's first governor, and he was promptly put on a ship to Virginia, accompanied by eight other ships with hundreds of new settlers. Sir Thomas Gates would not actually arrive in Virginia on this trip, as the fleet of ships was caught in a hurricane. His ship, specifically, was shipwrecked in Bermuda. However, the other ships did arrive, and the new settlers demanded that the president of Jamestown step down to make room for the newly-appointed governor. Although John Smith resisted the initial demand, he eventually gave in to the royal charter and was allowed to remain president until the governor arrived in Jamestown. John Smith would actually return to England in September (earlier than necessary) following a gunpowder accident, and within a month, the new leader, George Percy, had arrived and taken leadership of the colony until Sir Thomas Gates could arrive. John Smith would visit America one final time in 1614, when he would attempt and fail to colonize the area he named New England.

Although the Powhatan Chiefdom had mostly stopped supplying the settlers with food after Pocahontas relayed her father's threats to John Smith, the two groups had maintained a stable trade relationship, which had helped to fill the gaps in the settlers' diets. But Henry Spelman, Thomas Savage, and John Smith were gone, and Pocahontas had married another member of her own tribe. The Powhatan Paramount Chiefdom now had little connection to the Jamestown colony. Just after John Smith's departure from America, the Powhatan Paramount Chiefdom, under orders from Chief Powhatan, ended all relationship with the settlers, and the two groups acted as if they had never even had a relationship to begin with.

The settlers and the Native Americans were no longer allowed to trade, and although no formal notice of this decision was made to the Englishmen, any colonists who attempted to trade with a member of the Powhatan tribes were attacked. To make matters even worse, the Powhatan tribes started to become defensive of their territory. Although they allowed the settlers to keep Jamestown, the Native Americans were instructed to attack or even kill any settler they found hunting outside of Jamestown's fort. As the group had been dependent on the Native Americans' help, trade, and territory for food since its arrival, Jamestown suffered from a horrendous famine over the winter months.

The period from the end of 1609 to the subsequent winter of 1610 became known as the "Starving Time," as the settlers suffered from very little sustenance. Although the Jamestown residents tried to fill the serious gaps in their diets by eating their pets (dogs and cats), labor animals (horses), and local, sometimes diseased small game (rats and mice), there just wasn't enough food for the colonists. In their desperation, the most extreme residents attempted to eat shoe leather, and some even turned to cannibalism. By March of 1610, only a few months after the "Starving Time" began, less than 100 colonists remained of the 500 people noted in autumn of 1609. Hundreds had died of starvation, around forty had managed to escape Jamestown on a European ship, and only sixty or so settlers remained of a once-impressive first settlement.

During the "Starving Time," Sir Thomas Gates and his fellow shipmates who had been shipwrecked in Bermuda had managed to repair their two ships and were slowly making their way to Virginia under the leadership of Gates and George Somers. Finally, on May 24, 1610, when it seemed that the Jamestown settlement was simply going to die out and fail as the previous British colonies in America had, Sir Thomas Gates and Somers arrived to find a starving population of only a few dozen people. Sir Thomas Gates and George Somers had been expecting a stable, flourishing colony, as they had been informed Jamestown was when they departed England in the summer of 1609, and they were not prepared to essentially save the dying colony—especially as they had barely survived the trip to Virginia themselves. After only a month and a half in Jamestown, Gates and Somers and their fellow shipmates decided to abandon Jamestown. They boarded their ships to return to England with the remaining Jamestown colonists who wanted to join. The group did not make it far, as before they had even exited the Chesapeake Bay into the Atlantic Ocean, they were greeted by three English ships led by Thomas West. On them were 150 settlers and a sufficient food supply to feed the colonists. Gates and Somers were ordered to turn their ships around and return to Jamestown.

When they had returned to Jamestown, Gates was informed that he was not to take charge of the colony and that Thomas West had instead been appointed as governor of Virginia. Thomas West took charge immediately by contacting Chief Powhatan and requesting not only that the Powhatan Chiefdom return the weapons and tools that had been stolen from the settlement but also that the tribe turn over the Native American who had recently been accused of unfairly killing one of the previous settlers. Chief Powhatan refused to meet Thomas West's demands and threatened the colonists, warning them to stay within their allotted Jamestown peninsula—or, better yet, to leave the area altogether. That hostile response would launch a war between the two groups that had likely been a long time coming. The next year or so represented another difficult period for both the settlers and the Powhatans, as they had many minor conflicts and both groups suffered from diseases. The Powhatans were hit worse since they had little immunity against European diseases. In 1611, Governor Thomas West returned to England on Captain Samuel Argall's ship after suffering from various diseases. He was replaced by Sir Thomas Dale.

After returning to Virginia, Captain Samuel Argall was searching for food in the Potomac when he made contact with the Patawomecks, the tribe that Henry Spelman had moved to. After making contact with their chief, Japazeus, Argall became the first settler since John Smith to have positive relations with one of the Native American tribes. Samuel Argall was informed by his new allies that Pocahontas had been visiting the Patawomeck tribe. Knowing her importance to the Powhatan Paramount Chiefdom, with whom the settlers were currently at war, Argall plotted to kidnap her. Before long, with the help of Japazeus (whom Argall had pleaded to help him), the English captain had managed to kidnap Pocahontas (only fourteen-year-old at this time), and she returned with him to Jamestown as a prisoner, where she had not been since she had warned John Smith of her father's threats years before.

In Jamestown, Samuel Argall and his men attempted to use Pocahontas as a bargaining chip, demanding that, as ransom, the Powhatans return the weapons and tools they had taken from the settlers, as well some Englishmen they had taken as prisoners that year. However, Chief Powhatan did not take the bait. Before long, discussions and negotiations for Pocahontas' safe return to her father ended, and the Englishmen were left with the fourteen-year-old girl. As Jamestown had little use for Pocahontas, they sent her to Henricus, a newly-founded outpost just outside of present-day Richmond, Virginia, where she was forced to convert to Christianity. During her time in Henricus, Pocahontas was greatly admired by an Englishman named John Rolfe.

Virginia's Tobacco Industry

John Rolfe had actually been on one of the two ships that had shipwrecked on Bermuda on their way to Virginia in 1609. Like Sir Thomas Gates and George Somers, he did not arrive in Jamestown until 1610. In subsequent years, he began experimenting with growing tobacco, which was in widespread demand in Europe in the 17th century. Although Virginia had its own native tobacco crop, its bitterness did not suit the European's palette. After experimenting with different tobacco varieties, he finally attempted to grow a seed known as *Nicotiana tabacum*, which he had brought from the Orinoco River valley in the West Indies. It was an immediate success. The West Indies seed's tobacco was more palatable for the Englishmen, and when grown in the James River, it developed a unique and distinctive flavor.

In the summer of 1613, John Rolfe sent the first batch of his tobacco to England, where it was almost immediately beloved and in high demand. John Rolfe not only established the tobacco industry in Virginia but also established the first profitable industry in the future United States of America, launching the not-yet-formed country's capitalistic future. Rolfe became somewhat of a hero, as John Smith had been only a few years before. His tobacco profits inspired hope in the dying colony, giving them jobs that would yield profitable results. Within the next year, Virginia was producing enough tobacco to satisfy the United Kingdom's demands and compete with Spanish tobacco producers who had established their tobacco supply over decades. Following John Rolfe's success, many of the other colonists would grow their own tobacco crops, and over the next years, tobacco would spread all over Virginia. Tobacco would remain the colony's only profitable crop for the next decade and would be the most profitable source of income for Virginia for the following century.

Meanwhile, as John Rolfe attempted to grow his tobacco crop, his admiration for Pocahontas grew, as did Pocahontas' apparent connection to the Christian faith. While it is still debated whether her open appreciation for Christianity was truthful, forced, or planned, Pocahontas would fully convert to Christianity over the months after her kidnapping, under the instruction of Alexander Whitaker. Pocahontas quickly became somewhat of a spokesperson for conversion to the other Native Americans, and she openly renounced her own people's cultures and ideologies in favor of her new beliefs. By the beginning of 1614, Pocahontas would be publicly baptized, taking the Christian name Rebecca. According to documents written by Sir Thomas Dale, the governor of Virginia at the time, all of Pocahontas' changes were completely voluntary. Following Pocahontas' baptism, John Rolfe's admiration would culminate in his proposal of marriage, and in April of 1614, the two would be married. After the hostility between the colony and the Powhatans that had followed Pocahontas' kidnapping, the two groups would have a period of peace.

After her marriage, Pocahontas moved into Jamestown, and it is believed that her knowledge of agriculture is what enabled John Rolfe to successfully grow and harvest his tobacco crop. Soon after the wedding, Rolfe and Pocahontas would have their first child, whom they named Thomas Rolfe. During their relationship, the tobacco crop would prosper and supply enough tobacco for the British—to the extent that smoking was no longer a luxury but a commodity that all could afford to enjoy. As the couple had managed to save the colony from absolute starvation and create massive profits for the Virginia Company, Rolfe, Pocahontas, and Thomas were invited to London to speak of their successes and receive congratulations from the royal court. The trio arrived in London in the spring of 1616, where they were treated like royalty and attended elite ceremonies held in their honor.

However, despite Pocahontas being a guest of honor, the trip would end in catastrophe as Pocahontas fell sick. In 1617, at only twenty years old, she passed away due to the poor air and water quality in London, as she was not accustomed to the city's pollution. Since young Thomas was quite sick from the city's contaminated air and water, as well, John Rolfe left him with his uncle (Rolfe's brother), as it was not likely he would have survived the trip home. Thomas would survive and eventually return to America as an adult in 1640. Rolfe would return home soon after Pocahontas' death. After informing the Powhatan Paramount Chiefdom of the tragedy which had befallen the chief's daughter, the harmonious period came to an end. Although tensions rose, the two groups would remain peaceful for the next few years, however.

Chapter 4 – Virginia's Establishment as a Royal Colony (1619-1642)

Once Virginia began making strides towards being an economic success for the United Kingdom, the British government and the Virginia Company felt it was time to devote more attention to their American colony. In mid-1619, Britain instituted a representative democracy in Virginia, which until that point had been run by a single governor and a small governing council. This meant that citizens of Jamestown—at this time, only men who owned property—would have the right to vote for representatives who would form a proper General Assembly that would vote on the important decisions of the colony. At this point, Virginia was essentially divided into four boroughs, each of which would elect two representatives known as burgesses. In addition to the eight burgesses, the colony's seven plantations each chose two representatives, and the Virginia Company assembled six of its own representatives. Altogether, there were a total of twenty-eight burgesses in Virginia's General Assembly, which officially commenced on July 30, 1619. Although the General Assembly would have the right to vote on Virginia's laws and enactments, all decisions could be vetoed by the governor of Virginia and the Virginia Company, still located in London.

The introduction of a representative government was not the only major change the United Kingdom made to Virginia that year. Just after the formation of the General Assembly, the Virginia Company sent a ship full of women to the colony. The women, who came to be known as "tobacco brides," were traded to the farmers by the Virginia Company in exchange for pounds of tobacco (usually at least over 100 pounds). Many of the women were quite young, ranging from teenage to late 20s, and many had lost their fathers or both their parents, making their lives difficult in England. In Jamestown, the women were married to tobacco farmers and promptly birthed babies to help grow the colony. Since many of the women were ill-prepared for the conditions of life in Virginia, only a few dozen of the more than one hundred tobacco brides would survive more than a few years in the American colony.

Debatably more impactful than the arrival of the tobacco brides in 1619 was the arrival of slaves that same year. The first slaves of Virginia were actually not supposed to be sent to Virginia at all, as they were being sent to Mexico from Portugal. However, while in the West Indies, a Portuguese slave ship was attacked by Dutch and English pirates, who brought the slaves to the nearest British colony of Jamestown to sell. Although records detailing the transactions and lives of the African American slaves are in short supply, it is believed around twenty slaves were sold in Jamestown and began working on Virginia tobacco farms immediately to help meet the growing British demand, perhaps as indentured servants rather than slaves (meaning they would work for a specific time period rather than for life.

Growing Tensions with the Powhatan Paramount Chiefdom

Although no war had been declared following the death of Pocahontas in 1617 and the colony had remained overall peaceful with the Powhatan Paramount Chiefdom, tensions had been rising since John Rolfe's return. Pocahontas' father, the main reason the two groups had remained peaceful, passed shortly after his daughter, and the new chief of the Powhatan, Opechancanough, inherited an agitated tribe that resented the British colony. Finally, in 1622, animosity culminated when Opechancanough ordered an attack on the colony on March 22. The colonists—specifically, those in the plantations—were completely caught off guard, and 25-33 percent of Virginia's colonists died, including John Rolfe, whose massive tobacco plantation was completely destroyed.

Virginia Becomes England's First Royal Colony

Following the massacre, the colony and the Powhatan Paramount Chiefdom were officially at war, and the outcry in London and all of England was massive. This was no surprise, as England had just begun properly receiving profits and investing in its overseas colony. While the colony was directly dealing with the impact of the feud, decisions regarding the war were greatly debated between King James I and the royal assembly and the Virginia Company, the two groups finding it difficult to agree on a course of action since this was a matter of utmost importance.

After about a year of political disagreements, King James I sent a royal commission to investigate the Virginia Company and their decisions regarding Virginia. During the investigation, it was discovered that company officials had been taking advantage of the generous freedoms of their original charter to pad their salaries. This illegal practice had continued even as the tobacco industry tanked and the company faced bankruptcy. Upon receiving the report, King James I attempted to negotiate a new charter for the colony. Virginia Company swiftly refused the new charter.

After another year of disagreements, the king finally dissolved the Virginia Company altogether on May 24, 1624, and took complete control of Virginia. Virginia became England's first royal colony, with Jamestown as its official colonial capital. Although the main source of disagreement between the monarch and the Virginia Company had been the threat the Powhatan Chiefdom posed following the massacre of 1622, the colony's General Assembly, governor, and the Powhatans continued to war without any real instruction or help from the monarchy. On March 5, 1625, King James I passed away, and his successor, Charles I, would revoke the General Assembly's official legislation—despite the fact that the General Assembly had helped lead the colony's war efforts while the Virginia Company and the monarch debated on what to do. In October of 1626, the Powhatans and the colonists would finally negotiate a peace treaty to end their brutal war, which had killed several hundred people on both sides. The treaty, which would bring the two groups more than a decade of peace, detailed a border that would separate the colony's territory from the Powhatans' to prevent further conflict.

Over the course of the next decade, the colony would rebuild itself from the damages of war, which had wiped out many of its large plantations. Meanwhile, the monarchy of England reorganized Virginia's political structure, attempting to find a system that would work best for the colony and a leader who would help breathe new life into the colony after the devastating Anglo-Powhatan War. While reorganizing Virginia's political structure, the king sent clergymen to Virginia to impose taxes, handle the colony's finances, and govern the colonists. In the mid-1630s, the king of England split up Virginia into eight shires, later known as counties, each of which had its own representative clergymen. England would continue to send settlers to help grow the colony's population, many of whom were poor in England and would remain poor in Virginia, creating a large financial disparity between the rich, elite tobacco farmers, the middle class established citizens, and the poor new arrivals.

Chapter 5 – Virginia During the Sir William Berkeley Administrations (1642–1677)

The Sir William Berkeley Administration

There is little documentation about the early history of Virginia and even less documentation of the colony during the beginning of the 17th century, when much of the focus was on growing the colony and little of historical significance occurred. One notable change Virginia underwent during this period was the appointment of Sir William Berkeley as the governor in 1642. Sir William Berkeley, an Englishman who was new to Virginia, felt that exploration should be one of the colony's primary focuses in order to spread colonies around the territory and claim more land for England. For the first time since the foundation of Jamestown, the colony attempted to explore more of Virginia, focusing specifically on the rugged Trans-Allegheny region, which is mostly encompassed by the Appalachian Mountains. Sir William Berkeley also attempted to grow Virginia's economy. He encouraged tobacco farms to spread out, extending their territory right up to the Powhatan border, and he also attempted to introduce new profitable crops.

The Third Anglo-Powhatan War

Of course, the Powhatan Chiefdom, which had only a decade before instituted borders around its territory, was not pleased with the colony's explorations. Tensions grew as the two groups encountered each other in the Appalachians. On April 18, 1644, after almost two years of the colony's continued exploration, Chief Opechancanough launched a full-on attack on the British colony—this one far more bloody than the massacre in 1622. Once again, the Powhatans focused mainly on attacking the plantations, which were much less prepared for assaults than Jamestown, and it is estimated they wiped out around 500 colonists. This would mark the commencement of the Third Anglo-Powhatan War.

Over the next two years, the colonists would engage in a violent and bloody war with the Powhatan Chiefdom, and although the Powhatans had the initial advantage due to their surprise attack, the colonists would prove to be far more prepared for the war. Before long, the colonists had depleted and demolished much of the Powhatan Paramount's resources. In 1646, Opechancanough was captured by the colonists, forced into captivity, and killed. With the depletion of their resources on top of the death of their leader, the rest of the Powhatan Paramount Chiefdom, led by their new chief, Necotowance, realized they had little chance of overcoming the colonists' forces. After two years of warring, the two groups agreed to a peace treaty, which introduced new borders. The Powhatans were now restricted to just north of the York River, dividing their already divided land into an even smaller section.

Although Sir William Berkeley's attempts to explore Virginia were put on pause during The Third Anglo-Powhatan War, upon the formation of the peace agreement, the administration promptly returned to its explorations, and before long, new trading routes were formed, spanning from the Native Americans' territory in the southwest to what would eventually become the towns of Richmond and Petersburg. After the war, Sir William Berkeley continued his attempt to expand Virginia's profits, population, and capabilities by experimenting with new crops. Although none would overtake the success of Rolfe's tobacco plant, the focus on diversification and manufacturing would help strengthen Virginia's economy overall.

The Arrival of the Puritans

Although Sir William Berkeley would spend twenty-seven years as governor of Virginia, his terms would not be consecutive. Despite all of Berkeley's efforts and time spent in Virginia, he would remain a staunch loyalist to the Crown. While Sir William Berkeley was fighting threats from the Powhatans and nearby Dutch explorers and settlers, back in his homeland, they were fighting the English Civil War. Even in Virginia, Berkeley and the colonists proclaimed their loyalty to King Charles II, inviting all other loyalists to immigrate to Virginia for asylum. Virginia's population quickly grew with Royalists immigrating to the colony. However, when the English Civil War came to an end on September 3, 1651, as a victory for the Parliamentarians, the colony's open support of Charles II and the Royalists in the English Civil War would place them on the wrong side of history. Within the next year, Sir William Berkeley would be forced to retire when the parliamentary commissioners arrived aggressively in Virginia. Although during the years of Parliamentarian rule in England, Virginia was governed by the Parliament, little changed or advanced in the colony at all.

The Second Sir William Berkeley Administration

In 1659, when the Parliament was disbanded and, soon after, the monarchy restored in England, Berkeley returned to the position of governor, continuing his governorship until his death in 1677. Although Berkeley's first period as governor was plagued by the catastrophic Third Anglo-Powhatan War, he had an overall successful term as governor, as he had managed to propel the expansion of the colony. His second period as governor would be plagued with many difficulties. Although none would be as disastrous as the effects of the Third Anglo-Powhatan War, they would slow the development of

Virginia. The need for additional defense, combined with successive poor growing seasons, various diseases that plagued both humans and animals, and new high taxes from trade laws, forced Virginia into an economic depression and a difficult period the likes of which they had not seen since the "Starving Time."

Though the Powhatans and the colony had signed a peace treaty in 1646, and the colony was peaceful with other tribes overall, the Native Americans and the settlers continued to battle over the course of the 1660s and 1670s, forcing Berkeley to put a pause on expansion and exploration altogether to defend the colony from Native American attacks. Although Berkeley had some loyal admirers, there was growing discontent among the colony, which felt he was not doing all he could to help Virginia—specifically, in his attitude towards the Native Americans' attacks.

As the colonists tried to solve their economic issues by gradually expanding their territory, creating additional plantations for tobacco and other crops, they kept encroaching on the Native Americans' territory. Although Native American attacks were becoming more frequent, Berkeley held the opinion that it was best for the colony to refrain from warring with its neighbors, as war would only cause more economic issues, and it would be beneficial to foster trade relations with the various tribes. As Berkeley refused to stand up to the threat, a growing number of colonists disagreed with the governor's decisions. Before long, a rebellion group formed, led by Berkeley's cousin by marriage, Nathaniel Bacon.

In 1676, without Berkeley's approval, Nathaniel Bacon led an attack against the Native Americans. Although Governor William Berkeley threatened to use all forces necessary to stop them, Bacon and his group trudged on, which forced Berkeley to stay true to his word. Bacon and his rebellion group battled with Berkeley and his loyalists in the first inter-colony war, in which Bacon died of natural causes. Following the death of Bacon, Berkeley publicly hung many of the rebellion's more notable members, which finally caught King

Charles II of England's attention. Although Berkeley was sent to England to explain to the king all the dramatic events that had occurred during his governorship, Berkeley died shortly after arriving, before he had the chance to speak to the king to whom he had remained so loyal through his time in Virginia. Just after Berkeley left Virginia for England, King Charles II signed a treaty with multiple Virginian Native American tribes, known as the Treaty of 1677, which promised that the tribes would be loyal to the British Crown in order to keep their protected territories and remain protected from future attacks while continuing to migrate to fish and hunts.

Chapter 6 – The Century Leading Up to Virginia's Independence (1677–1751)

After Berkeley's Administration

Berkeley's successive governors were quite successful in expanding not only Virginia's territory but also its economy, culture, and politics. Although Bacon's rebellion was short-lived, the sentiment of distrust for the governors—specifically, those loyal to the Crown—continued. The yearning for a separate government from the English monarchy grew as Virginia continued to develop its own unique culture and population. Although Virginians had been promised in their original charter that they would enjoy all the liberties of English citizens, Virginia dealt with aggressive taxation, trade regulations, and vetoes on any dissent to laws imposed by the Crown, all of which helped fuel the growing discontent.

While the colony of Virginia was prospering and cultivating its independence, the Native Americans were struggling to survive. The various wars had taken a toll on the tribes—specifically, the Powhatans, who had suffered the most from battles with the colonists. However, war was not the primary threat the Native Americans faced from the colony. Rather, it was the diseases brought to America from Europe that would take so many of the first peoples' lives. As the Native Americans had existed without these diseases for their entire lives, they simply had no immunity or resistance to the illnesses. (Recall how Pocahontas died shortly after breathing in English air and drinking polluted London water.) Although there is little documentation of the Native American population of Virginia at that time, and what exists is likely inaccurate, it is estimated to have decreased by tens of thousands in less than a hundred years since the first settlement of Jamestown.

Virginian Colonists' Continued Expansion

A lot had changed since the first days of struggle for the colonists in Virginia, and over the course of the 17th century, the colony continued to advance in more ways than one. Although in almost every colony in America there was a focus on educating the Native Americans in order to convert them to Christianity, in Virginia, an education system for the non-native population is believed to have been set up as early as 1621. The system for white children, known as the "East India School," was intended to be a "publique [public] free school for the education of children and grounding them in the principles of religion, civility of life and humane learning." In other words, Virginia may have had the earliest example of public schooling in the future United States of America and perhaps even the world. A few years before that, in 1618, the colony had, in fact, obtained a royal charter allowing them to form a university in Virginia. However, that would not be achieved until the end of the 17th century, as the proposed land for what was to be named the University of Henrico became the grounds for much of the Anglo-Powhatan Wars.

Regardless of the delay in constructing a university, Virginia was quickly becoming cultured. Finally, in 1693, the opening of the College of William & Mary in the town of Williamsburg, Virginia, would reflect that. The College of William & Mary, named for King William III and Queen Mary II, would be the second-oldest institution of higher education in all of the United States, after Harvard University. The opening of Virginia's first college would help the colony's progression into the intellectually advanced and modern world, giving it a reason to feel deserving of more independence. In other words, the colony that had spent decades focused solely on surviving was allowed for the first time to advance its culture and minds, as had been a right in England for generations.

Although the College of William & Mary had to be approved by the Crown and the governor of Virginia, the entire operation was funded, constructed, and opened by the elite Virginians who had in many ways overpowered the colony's local government. Clergyman James Blair, a perfect example of one of Virginia's elite, was a cofounder of Virginia's first college. Although he had no true political power, he would have enough influence to remove three separate leaders from governorship.

Similar to the political sphere, the economy was dominated entirely by tobacco plantation owners. While "tobacco brides" were a concept in early Virginia's history, by the latter half of the 17th century, women were no longer sent over from England simply to have children and populate the colony. Marriage became an important strategy for elite families to add more importance to their name and thereby increase their control, similar to how it was within royal families in Europe. Dances and other joyous celebrations became traditional for the wealthy few in Virginia, who used parties to introduce younger members of their families and forge business relationships. Although the elite had few obstacles to keeping their superior position in society, much of their riches were built from the ever-important tobacco crops, which occasionally had less than favorable seasons. As the economy was entirely based on one crop, it was not uncommon for rich tobacco plantation owners to have debts with British merchants who expected certain quantities every season— all of which was taxed heavily, decreasing the colonists' profits. These factors helped fuel the Virginian elite's dissatisfaction with not only the British merchants but also the Crown and the local government.

Much like other societies in the world, the measure of riches in Virginia quickly became about family name (adding more importance to strategic marriages) and displayed material objects (large homes, large plantations). But another important measure of wealth in Virginia had to do with the number of slaves one owned. While some African slaves had arrived in America as early as 1619, for most of the 17th century, it was generally uncommon for plantations to have slaves. If they had slaves, they were almost entirely white. However, this statistic would gradually change. By the 1690s, there were four times as many African slaves as white ones, and that number would only continue to grow over the coming years as owning slaves became more affordable. Of course, as the future Civil War would indicate, owning slaves became a fundamental right in Virginia—officially so with the act known as the Slave Code of 1705. Although purchasing slaves was not cheap, it was seen as an investment for plantation owners. There was little consideration for the lives of the slaves, as purchasing slaves was seen much like purchasing a tractor to replace hand-picking crops would be seen today.

By the turn of the millennium, while Virginia was still under colonial rule, it had internally established itself as different from England, with its own culture, ideologies, and systems. As elite families joined together and plantation owners had access to slaves to speed up their production, the elite families' wealth grew, allowing plantations to expand at record rates. This forced Virginia, in general, to expand rapidly. However, although Virginia was advancing at an incredible speed, especially with the creation of its college, there was still one factor holding it back, and that was the town that started it all: Jamestown.

Due to the seepage of salt water into the waterways surrounding Jamestown, the drinking water had become contaminated. To make matters worse, much of the population of Jamestown was on the poorer side, as most of the rich plantation owners lived in rural areas where they could expand their farms. Since the population of Jamestown was mostly made up of incoming immigrants and poor Virginians, living conditions were quite poor, and diseases introduced by immigrants and poor eating habits spread like wildfire. Speaking of fire, Jamestown had been burnt down multiple times. Since the buildings were constructed with cheap materials (wood), the entire town had been destroyed. This explains why it was mostly inhabited by lower-income families. By the end of the 17th century, Jamestown was no longer a suitable capital city. After much discussion, it was decided the capital should be moved to Williamsburg, the home of the College of William and Mary. Topped with the fact that Williamsburg had a higher elevation that would allow Virginians to better protect themselves from any incoming threats, Williamsburg seemed to be the perfect place for Virginia's capital city. In 1699, the capital city was officially moved from the town that started Virginia (and America) to Williamsburg, just over ten kilometers away—a not-too-drastic move.

Virginia at the Beginning of the 18th Century

By the beginning of the 18th century, Virginia would have the largest population of all the American colonies, and by the time of the American Revolution, its population would have grown to over 120,000 people. Although there was still, of course, a large wealth disparity between plantation owners and those living in poor conditions, the population of Virginia was an overall sophisticated one, and much of the population had the opportunity for upward momentum in one form or another. While the colony was still almost entirely dependent on the tobacco crop, this shining crop had managed to improve its economic situation, as the demand for tobacco only increased. However, as with any type of agriculture, there comes a point when repeated farming of the same crop wears down the soil. As tobacco crops began underperforming due to the need to rest the soil, plantation owners began searching for new land.

Since Virginia had already claimed all the eastern land up to the Atlantic Ocean (with Native Americans and a growing new colony to the south and other French and British colonies to the north), it was forced to expand westward towards the Piedmont and the Blue Ridge. Throughout the 18th century, the Virginian's search for land took them as far as Ohio (which now borders West Virginia), where plantation owners had some hostile run-ins with French settlers.

As Virginia's elite increased their wealth in the form of property ownership and eventual profits, their influence on politics continued to grow. Although a Crown-selected governor and a governor's council remained, the House of Burgesses (which had been introduced with representative democracy in 1619) was gaining power and slowly overtaking the political members actually in charge. The House of Burgesses became a form of opposition to the royal prerogatives, and although its power did not technically equal that of the royally-appointed governor and governor's council, the House of Burgesses began to represent a second political party—one which favored the people of Virginia rather than the British Crown. Though only a few decades before, Sir William Berkeley had remained so faithful to England's monarchy, that loyalty was quickly vanishing among the colonists. While some older members of the population remained royalists, the younger generations were trending towards demanding independence.

In the years that preceded the American Revolution, Virginia would continue to forge its own culture, one that strayed from English culture and began to resemble much of what we, in modern times, imagine when we think of the old South. Even though plantation owning was rather new, the concept of old money—in other words, powerful families who stayed rich generationally—was becoming cemented into society as early as the 18th century. Of course, as conditions improved for plantation owners, they worsened for slaves.

At the start of the 18th century, almost all Virginian slaves were born in Africa, but that fact was beginning to change. By the 1770s, more than 90 percent of Virginian slaves would be born in Virginia. Yet, despite the slaves sharing the same birthplace as their masters, slaves were allowed neither the liberties of an Englishman in England during colonial rule nor the freedoms of an American citizen after the revolution. Although there were some free African Americans in Virginia, some of which even owned slaves, they received almost no respect from the white Virginians. In 1723, the assembly would even go as far as to deny them the right to vote.

As even free Africans had trouble integrating with the white Virginians, they began to develop their own culture separate from the white colonists, just as white Virginians had developed their own culture inspired by, yet separate from, their home country of England. Africans in Virginia developed their own traditions, ideologies, religious beliefs, forms of communication and storytelling, music, and more from their home countries.

Despite the fact that slavery would continue to be common in Virginia for more than a century, there were attempted revolts as early as the 17th century, much of which ended in public hangings. Overall, slavery would become intrinsically tied to Virginia's (white) American culture, as plantation owners used slaves to not only grow their profits but also display their wealth. Although the British Crown did not oppose slavery at all, there were some cases—such as the decision to deny free Africans the right to vote—the British Crown would view as excessive, thus alienating Virginians even more from their English ancestors.

Another aspect of Virginia's culture that would change drastically in the 18th century was religion. As with almost every colony, religion was a principal purpose behind colonization. Missions had the goal of converting the native population to Christianity, as was apparent with the conversion of Pocahontas. The Church of England played an important role in the formation of Virginia, especially during the 1630s when the politics and economy of Virginia were run by English clergymen. Since the Church played such a large role in the politics of

Virginia, all colonists were legally enforced to not only attend every religious service but also help fund the Church. Since attending church was mandatory, services quickly became important in Virginia's society, as they offered colonists the chance to forge connections with other colonists who perhaps lived a distance away. Subsequently, church was used as not only a place of worship but also a place to create economic, social, and political relationships and to discuss news, gossip, and the economy. In other words, the church became intrinsically tied to almost every aspect of society.

Although Virginia's church was Anglican Protestant, over the 18th century, different Protestant groups began to appear—namely, Baptists, Methodists, and Presbyterians. Since the church had become a home for elite Virginians to forge business, political, and social relationships, these new forms of religion attracted poor and middle-class Virginians who still felt an attachment towards Christianity but no particular loyalty toward Anglican Christianity. Over the next decades, these other religious options would begin to pull in wealthy Virginians, as well. Before long, one's religious affiliation could potentially affect one's friendships, business partners, future spouse, and more.

While Virginia's churches were not much different in the 18th century than they are today, they did certainly push ideologies that were relevant at that time. One of those ideologies was the place of women in society. Overall, the role of a woman in Virginia's society was to be a good, supportive wife who cooked, cleaned, entertained, and—most importantly—bore children for her husband. While there were some poorer women who worked on the tobacco plantations, it was generally considered to be unladylike for women to work. This helped to further the bias against slaves, many of whom were, of course, women who had little choice of whether they worked. Enforcing the belief that women who worked were unladylike and not dignified helped solidify the narrative that women slaves were less woman-like and, in many ways, not comparable to a white woman in society.

Though there were some white women who managed to open businesses—namely taverns, or in some rare cases like Margaret Brent, plantations—such was not the norm. Women whose behaviors contradicted the expectations of Virginia's churches were often accused of being witches, a charge which usually resulted in death. Although white women, Africans, and Native Americans' rights were totally in the hands of the rich and powerful white male Virginians, they ironically felt that British colonial rule was restrictive and that they should have their own authority in their homeland.

As with many rebellions, much of the political discussions which would lead to the revolution occurred among the educated college students who had open forums in which to cover various topics, many of which surrounding what they believed should be the freedoms and rights of a Virginian citizen. Since most university students were children of Virginia's elite who generally did not favor the strict taxation and regulations imposed on their exports, it would come as no surprise that the educated would become the leaders of the revolution. For example, Thomas Jefferson's father owned a rather large plantation with over sixty slaves, and his mother was related to one of the more prominent wealthy families in Virginia. Jefferson grew up attending school, leading him perfectly to his future as a student at the College of William & Mary, which he began attending in 1760.

The years preceding Jefferson's (and the other future founding fathers') college years would give the future students plenty to discuss, as the English government and Virginian elite disagreed on many policies. Just one example of the many disagreements is the 1751 pistole fee dispute, in which the British decided to uphold the Virginian governor's right to charge one pistole (around eighteen shillings) on land grants if he decided to attach a colony seal to them. While this amount was not excessive for the wealthy Virginians who owned land, it was the principle that the governor could demand unnecessary money if he felt like declaring the land in question colony land.

Chapter 7 – Virginia's Independence and the Formation of the United States of America (1751–1783)

Although Virginia's demand for independence was inevitable, the events of the French and Indian War (1754–1763) certainly sped up the process, as it forced Virginians to take serious action against the British Crown. While the British and the French fought the Seven Years' War back in Europe, their hostility was also expressed in the Americas, where their colonies fought their own war. While the French had been inhabiting the Americas just as long as the English, their settlements (mostly in present-day Canada) could not compare to those that had been built in the modern-day United States, where the British colonies outnumbered the French settlements by hundreds of thousands of people. While the war was mainly between the French colonies and the English colonies, the war was titled the French and Indian War since both sides were strongly supported by various groups of Native Americans.

Although the war occurred mostly around the present Canada-United States border, Virginia had quite a bit at stake, especially since much of the war was fought over Ohio, near which Virginia had spread many of its plantations. What's more, many wealthy Virginians had invested in the Ohio Company, which would be at a loss if the French took over Ohio. Virginia's military regiment was led by none other than George Washington, who was only twenty-one years old at the time but a major in the military. For the first time, the British colonies were forced to work together to fight against the French, forging a military relationship that would be beneficial later in the American Revolution.

Of course, as Canada is a mostly English country today, the war in America was a British success, as was that of the Seven Years' War back in Europe. Yet, despite England's success in both wars, upon the termination of the battles in 1763, the British Crown was left with an incredible amount of debt. To help pay off the large debt the British Crown had accumulated over the course of the two wars, it began to introduce new regulations, almost all of which included higher taxation rates on commonly imported and exported items. The most notable of these taxes were the Stamp Act and later the Tea Act.

The Stamp Act was introduced quickly after the end of the war as England's first attempt to collect money from its colonies to repay its war debt. The Stamp Act essentially required all legal documents, including college diplomas, marriage licenses, playing cards, pamphlets, contracts, newspapers, wills, and more to carry a stamp—not only in Virginia but also in all the British American colonies. Although some of the taxation placed on Virginians up to that date was excessive, the stamp duty was neither extreme nor unfair exactly, as it had been in place in England since 1694 and had proved to be a useful system for the government to collect revenue.

Despite the fact that the Stamp Act had already been in place in England, Virginia and the other British colonies were immediately and intensely opposed to the tax. The very first resistance to the tax would come from Virginia's House of Burgesses on May 29, 1765, when Patrick Henry and the House of Burgesses issued a series of five resolves in response to the law that would come to be known as the Virginia Resolves. The resolves were as follows: first and second, that Virginians should have as much freedom and equality as if they had been in England; third, that a government should not impose an unbearable tax on their people; fourth, that a tax should not be passed in Virginia if no Virginians had given their consent on the matter; and fifth, that only Virginia's General Assembly should have the right to impose taxes.

The first two resolves were quite similar to those in the original charter formed years before the creation of Virginia, and the final three resolves explained that the Stamp Tax would be unbearable to Virginians and the Crown should not have the right to pass taxes anymore— especially not without the approval of Virginia's General Assembly. Patrick Henry essentially aired what much of Virginia had been discussing for the last century. Before long, the resolves were published in newspapers, and word of the Virginia Resolves spread to the other American colonies. The phrase "No taxation without representation" became the slogan of the anti-Crown movement, essentially reiterating the fourth and fifth resolves—that people should not be required to pay a tax to a government they have no part in.

As the news of Virginia's daring resolves reached the other colonies, other colonial representatives began following suit and speaking out about their dissatisfaction towards the newly introduced Stamp Act. By the end of summer, the colony of Massachusetts had requested a meeting with representatives from all the British American colonies. Finally, in October of 1765, the group met in New York at a conference they titled the Stamp Act Congress. Of course, the colonies were upset about much more than just the Stamp Act, all of which was revealed and discussed at the Stamp Act Congress.

The Declaration of Rights and Grievances

By the end of the meeting, the group co-wrote a document titled the "Declaration of Rights and Grievances," which detailed fourteen points of concern, including but not limited to the Stamp Act. The first point confirmed that although the colonies were not in England or Europe, they were to be just as loyal to the British Crown and understand their placement below Parliament and the Crown, just as those born or living in England did. Similar to the original charter and the first two points of the Virginia Resolves, the second point detailed that those living in British colonies were entitled to the same rights and privileges as anyone born or living in Great Britain. The third point (also similar to as it was written in the Virginia Resolves) was that no taxes should be imposed on a people by a government in which they have no representation.

Continuing the last point, the fourth said that the people of the British Colonies were not to be represented in the House of Commons in Great Britain, as they could not be both a colony member and take part in the government in Great Britain. The fifth point clarified, as was written in the Virginia Resolves, that only colony representatives chosen by members of the colony could impose taxes. The sixth concern explained that Great Britain should no longer have access to free resources and supplies that were the property of the colonies, as it was not constitutional (according to the British constitution) or reasonable to take the property of the colonies without payment. The seventh point demanded that all British subjects in the colonies should have the right to a trial by jury.

As was the main intention of the meeting, the eighth point declared that the Stamp Tax, as well as some of the other acts recently put in place, violated the rights and liberties of British citizens that colonists were entitled to. The ninth point, continued from the eighth, explained that the taxes imposed by the recent Parliament acts would be burdensome and impractical for the colonists to pay. The tenth point went on to confirm that, while the colonies were looking for some independence, profits and trade would continue to center in Great Britain. The colonies would continue to pay manufacturers and contribute to the Crown's supplies. Similarly, the eleventh point confirmed that due to restrictive parliamentary acts, colony members would be unable to purchase manufactured goods from Great Britain.

The twelfth point detailed that free enjoyment of the colony members' rights and liberties, in addition to non-hostile intercourse with Great Britain, would be mutually necessary for the prosperity of the colonies. The thirteenth point declared that all British subjects in the American colonies had the right to petition both the houses of Parliament and the king if they felt it necessary. Finally, the fourteenth point stated: "that it is the indispensable duty of these colonies to the best of sovereigns, to the mother country, and to themselves, to endeavor, by a loyal and dutiful address to his majesty, and humble application to both houses of Parliament, to procure the repeal of the act for granting and applying certain stamp duties, of all clauses of any other acts of Parliament, whereby the jurisdiction of the admiralty is extended as aforesaid, and of the other late acts for the restriction of the American commerce." The Declaration of Rights and Grievances was sent to the king of England, who at this time was King George III, as well as to the House of Commons and the House of Lords.

However, while the colonies' representatives dealt with their issues through official petitions, the civilians (most of whom had little involvement in politics thus far) took to the streets to demonstrate in the form of protests, rallies, and in some cases, more violent riots. The demonstration groups assumed names proudly displaying their demands for freedom, including the Sons of Liberty and the Liberty Boys. For the most part, the groups were led by powerful elites in the colonies, some of which were tobacco farmers, but most of the leaders were local politicians, lawyers, and other men in society familiar with law and order. For example, the leader of the Boston Sons of Liberty, Samuel Adams (second cousin to John Adams, the future second president of America) briefly studied law, was a tax collector (until the introduction of the unfavorable taxes), and was involved in local politics. He, like most of the protesting groups' leaders, gained favor through ideologies and action rather than riches.

To get the attention of those associated with the implementation of the British taxes, the demonstrators created effigies (accurate models/mannequins) of the tax collectors and British representatives and then publicly hung the models where civilians—and, of course, the effigies' inspirations—could see. In the more violent protests, the stamp collectors and British representatives' homes were ransacked and their occupants covered in hot tar and feathers, which was a common public torture method used by mobs in Europe. Most of the stamp/tax collectors and British representatives feared for their safety and even their lives. Although these positions were quite high paying, most appointed to be stamp collectors would resign before even beginning their position to stay out of danger. To harm the British government even further, many of the civilians began boycotting British goods, and some of the more extreme protestors attempted to stop the importation of British goods to the colonies altogether.

It did not take long for news of the protests and violence to reach London, and as had become the norm in the discussions of what to do with the colonies, the people of England were divided in their opinions. Within the British Parliament, two main contradicting factions developed, each of which attracted their own considerable supporters. Great Britain's prime minister, Lord Rockingham, led the faction that supported keeping the Stamp Act and felt that repealing it would take away the power and supremacy of the British Parliament in the colonies. Some of the more extreme believers of this faction insisted there could be absolutely no ceding to any of the colonies' requests on the Declaration of Rights and Grievances.

The other faction, which believed that the Stamp Act should be repealed, had the support of powerful British Parliament members, as well, including William Pitt and Edmund Burke. Many of the supporters of the latter faction were British businessmen who were more ideologically aligned with the first faction's belief that repealing the Stamp Act would take away the power and supremacy of the British Parliament in the colonies but needed to align with the faction that intended to repeal the Stamp Act because the boycotting of British goods was putting a strain on their businesses.

One colony member who helped sway more Parliament members to support repealing the Stamp Act was Benjamin Franklin. Benjamin Franklin served as a perfect middleman for the colonies and England, as he was born in Boston, Massachusetts, and served on the Pennsylvania Assembly but was an adamant supporter of the British Parliament. He was even known to say that the British political structure was the greatest in the world. In 1757, Benjamin Franklin traveled to England on other business, and though he would return to America for two years between 1762-1764, he would promptly return to London, where he would live for eighteen years. While he had left America, he could hardly escape the American drama following the Stamp Act. Benjamin Franklin opposed the Stamp Act at first. However, unlike other civilians born in the colonies, once he saw the act was going through, he supported the inevitable duties and ordered stamps for his printing firm. Franklin was outwardly disgusted by the violent protests, riots, and mobs in America and was quoted as saying, "A firm Loyalty to the Crown and faithful Adherence to the Government of this Nation [...] will always be the wisest Course for you and I to take, whatever may be the Madness of the Populace or their blind Leaders." This, of course, was a favorable position for him while living in England, but his reputation was essentially ruined back in America.

Yet, Benjamin Franklin would recover his reputation in America enough to not only become a founding father of the country but also end up on the United States' future one hundred dollar bill. He did so by testifying before the British Parliament, explaining that the colonies would be willing to pay external taxes, such as those on imports and exports, and that the colonies only had an issue with internal taxes such as the Stamp Act. Benjamin Franklin returned to his original belief that the Stamp Act should be repealed, and he publicly denounced internal taxation on the colonies. Luckily, Franklin had acquired quite a favorable reputation while in England, as he had the power to sway not only many members of Parliament but also a very reluctant King George III to repeal the act.

Finally, in March of 1766, the Stamp Act was repealed. However, while the colonies celebrated, this would not be the end of oppressive colonial rule in America. On the very same day, the British Parliament passed an act that allowed them to pass any law over the colonies "in all cases whatsoever." Although Benjamin Franklin loved England and had no intention of returning to America, he began henceforth embracing his Americanness, as he put it, and attempted to bridge the gap between the English colonies and their monarchy, to no avail. Franklin would write over 100 newspaper articles discussing every side of the issues, attempting to explain the colonies' opinions to the British and the opposite, as well, but it would all be in vain. Before long, he became too British for the Americans and too American for the British to listen to.

The Townshend Acts

Although Benjamin Franklin did help repeal the Stamp Act, which required swaying a majority of the British Parliament, many members were still dissatisfied with the lack of authority they had over the colonies. They felt it was necessary to follow through on their newly introduced act that allowed the Parliament to pass any law over the colonies in all cases whatsoever. This exertion of power was first demonstrated in the introduction of the Townshend Acts, which were a series of four acts. The first act within the Townshend Acts was the Suspending Act in 1767 and 1768, which declared that until the New York Assembly complied with the 1765 Quartering Act (which required the colonies to financially support any and all British forces stationed in their colonies), they would no longer be allowed to conduct any business.

The second act, known as the Revenue Act, implemented further taxes on lead, glass, paper, paint, and tea. However, although Benjamin Franklin had declared that the colonies would be willing to pay external taxes, the colonies were not pleased with this second act, as it was not implemented to regulate trade but to simply display British superiority and raise England's revenue. The third act, once again seen as simply a display of British superiority, declared that there should be not only stricter enforcement but also greater numbers of those who enforced customs collections, such as officers, spies, coast guards, and other such implementers of British law.

Finally, the Townshend Act's fourth and final act, known as the Indemnity Act, would lower duties on England's East India Company's tea to help England's tea makers compete with the smuggled-in tea of the Dutch merchants. Since the East India Company and the British treasury's profits would be decreasing due to the lower duties on British tea, they would need to increase the duties on other products—and additional implementers of the law to ensure the duties were paid. Of course, the colonies were not satisfied with the implementation of the Townshend Acts, which took away even more of their liberties than the Stamp Act had. Civilians took to the streets once again to demonstrate their frustrations, and protests often became violent. At the time, it was considered heroic in the eyes of colony members to not pay the imposed duties and to be downright hostile towards British enforcement agents. Most of the Townshend Acts would actually be repealed in early 1770 due to the demonstrations.

The Tea Act

Although England had averted a full-fledged revolution in 1770 when it lifted the majority of the Townshend Acts, it left a few in place—specifically, the duties on tea. Although the Indemnity Act had attempted to secure the East India Company's place as the number one tea supplier in the colonies, the company was not able to compete with the Dutch smugglers who provided tea for the colonies at a fraction of the price. Although the Townshend Acts' duty on tea had remained intact to help the struggling British East India Company, the company continued to have serious fiscal issues and built up a storage of several million pounds of tea in England due to the reduced sales in the colonies. Since the British East India Company had a contract with the British government requiring them to pay 400,000 pound sterling (GBP) annually, the company had built up debt due to the lack of sales in the colonies. On top of this, economic issues occurring in India and France seriously affected the British East India Company's sales.

In an attempt to salvage the British East India Company from bankruptcy, the 1773 Tea Act was imposed on the colonies, which essentially sanctioned the British East India Company's monopoly on tea. Although no new duty was imposed, this Tea Act angered all of the colonies, who felt they should have access to different merchants without being forced to import a product only from England. Though the duty on tea had been in place since the Townshend Acts of 1767–68, the implementation of the 1773 Tea Act made the colonies feel that every shipment of tea was a symbol of Britain's oppressive rule, which would inevitably lead to further tyrannical acts and cruel taxes. While all the colonies openly demonstrated against the Tea Act, the most serious demonstration of dissatisfaction was the Boston Tea Party, where protesting colonists shouting "No taxation without representation!" dumped hundreds of chests of tea off a shipment boat into the harbor. Considering many of the British Parliament members were shareholders in the East India Company, the Boston Tea Party is often considered the action that truly set off the American Revolution.

The Intolerable Acts

In an effort to single out Massachusetts following the Boston Tea Party, the British Parliament introduced the Intolerable Acts (also known as the Coercive Acts) in 1774, which consisted of four acts. The first two acts attempted to punish Massachusetts—and, more specifically, Boston—by closing down their harbor, forbidding town meetings, and replacing their elected local council with one appointed by the Parliament. The third Intolerable Act was known as the Administration of Justice Act. This was similar to today's extradition laws, as it would allow British officials to be tried in England (or another colony) if they had been charged with a capital offense. This way, a hostile government could not unfairly convict someone they did not like. Finally, the fourth Intolerable Act forces the colonial government to arrange housing for British troops in their colony by offering up unoccupied buildings, similar to the laws presented during the Quartering Act.

Although the Intolerable Acts were not all that strict, especially in comparison with previously implemented acts, the colonies had no tolerance for any more British control over their people and territory, and almost every colony attempted to fight back in some way. Most colonies simply protested the Intolerable Acts, but in Boston, which had been the target of the strictest acts, civilians refused to allow the British troops to move into their unoccupied buildings by preventing the completion of the repairs that would make the abandoned buildings livable for the troops. While the Intolerable Acts attempted to single out Massachusetts and demonstrate England's superiority over colonies that did not want to respect their rules, introducing the acts had quite the opposite effect. Rather than make an example of Massachusetts, England pushed the colonies to use Massachusetts as further justification to fuel their dissatisfaction towards the monarchy and Parliament.

The First Continental Congress

Following the introduction of the Intolerable Acts in the spring of 1774, public dissatisfaction for England grew. For the second time in the colonies' history, there would be a mass meeting of the representatives to discuss their grievances towards the British Parliament and Crown and what should be done. On September 5, 1774, every colony but Georgia sent representatives, totaling fifty-six deputies, to Philadelphia, where they held the First Continental Congress. The congress elected Peyton Randolph as president, a Virginian lawyer who, like Benjamin Franklin, was somewhat of a bridge between the British Crown and the colonial civilians. The group elected Charles Thomson to be their secretary, and also present at the congress were George Washington, John and Samuel Adams, and other founding fathers of the United States of America. Although there were more representatives than colonies present, and some colonies had larger or older populations than others, each colony was accorded one vote to keep everything fair without altercations. Of course, the congress met in secret.

Although some of the group had originally intended to discuss how to live under British rule without any British authority present, the group's true belief in the need for complete colonial freedom became apparent. It would come as no surprise that some matters of great importance at the congress were the denunciation of taxation without representation, as well as the removal of the Quartering and Intolerable Acts. However, the congress desired more than just that. Throughout the meeting, the representatives formed a declaration of rights that would protect the lives, property, and the rights of assembly and trial by jury for all colonial civilians (which at that time referred to non-slave, non-Native American, and in most cases, non-female civilians).

While the congress was essentially demanding freedom from colonial rule, it did not intend to go to war altogether, so it decided not to request a change in Parliamentary regulation of trade. This would allow England to still benefit from its colony and keep some level of superior power. Also discussed at the First Continental Congress was how to force England to cede to its demands. In the end, the group decided to once again boycott British goods and cease all exportation of American goods to England and the other British colonies, except for rice. Finally, the First Continental Congress sent out its petition of demands and set a date of May 10, 1775, for the Second Continental Congress.

The First Battles of the American Revolution

Meanwhile, even before the meeting of the First Continental Congress, military clashes had begun between the colonial civilians—at first, those in Massachusetts—and the British military led by General Thomas Gage, the general of all British troops in the American colonies. As the Intolerable Acts stated, Massachusetts' elective local council was to be replaced by one appointed by the Parliament, which in this case was a military government led by Gen. Thomas Gage. Despite having a large task at hand, Gen. Thomas Gage was only accorded around 4,000 men to govern a hostile Massachusetts and prevent war, which was becoming inevitable throughout the resentful New England colonies. Throughout 1774, Gen. Thomas Gage and his troops traveled through New England, seizing war preparations such as stores of weapons.

Although the colonial civilians were caught off guard by the British troops at first, before long, they came to expect the arrival of troops and began hiding their supplies. Yet, the colonies had lost plenty of their weapons. Towards the end of the year, they decided they would need to strike back to restore their supplies. With much research and planning, various independence groups, notably the Sons of Liberties, uncovered the best British weapons supply store to ransack, which was the under-protected weapons store at Fort William and Mary in Portsmouth, New Hampshire. On December 14, 1774, hundreds of colonial men stormed Fort William and Mary and managed to seize most of the fort's supply of powder, cannons, and small arms. To further display their dissatisfaction with the Crown, they lowered the British flag at the fort, demonstrating that they no longer supported nor associated with the flag. By the beginning of 1775, the situation had essentially reversed for the colonial civilians and the British troops. In the first few months of the year, the colonial rebellion groups were seizing all the British troops' weapons and war supplies.

No matter how well the British troops attempted to hide their plans, the colonials were always one step ahead, gradually gaining superiority in their territory.

After months of continued hostilities, on April 14, 1775, Massachusetts officially declared it was in an open state of revolt, and in response, Gen. Thomas Gage was given orders to arrest and imprison colonial leaders, specifically those in Massachusetts who had been the most radical. Gen. Thomas Gage had planned to first travel to Lexington, where his troops would capture Massachusetts' colonial leaders and then continue on to Concord, where much of Massachusetts' gunpowder was stored. However, all did not go as planned. Once again, the British army's plans were intercepted by colonial independence groups.

On April 16, 1775, Paul Revere, a Boston native who had become somewhat of a hero in the revolutionary movement, rode to Concord to inform his fellow patriots and urge them to move the military supplies. After setting up a signal system in Boston, Revere traveled on a horse for hours straight throughout the colony to warn as many as possible about the plans of the British. When the British troops arrived in Lexington on April 19th, expecting to capture the colonial leaders by surprise, the colonial forces were ready for the attack. Although the colonial forces were a fraction of the British army's forces, only seven Americans died at the face-off in Lexington. Then the British moved on to take Concord, where they were surprised to find that the weapons had been moved and the colonial forces were prepared for battle. At Concord, the British army was actually outnumbered. In the end, the Battle of Lexington and Concord had killed and wounded only ninety-five Americans in comparison to 273 British, forcing the British to realize that they had, in fact, lost their position of power in their American colonies.

The Second Continental Congress

Following the Battle of Lexington and Concord, no one could deny that the American revolutionary movement was in full swing. As both England and the Continental Congress planned the best military approach, troops from both sides converged in Boston. The members of the Second Continental Congress remained mostly the same, with the addition of Thomas Jefferson and Benjamin Franklin. Although the battles had been mostly centered around Massachusetts, at the Second Continental Congress, the colonies decided that the New England military forces that had been fighting and converging in Boston represented all of the colonies. Hence, the congress formed the first official American army. The Second Continental Congress officially named Virginia native George Washington chief of the American army, as he had proven his military prowess while leading the Virginia military regiment in the French and Indian War at only twenty-one years old. He was to take over the military forces on June 15, 1775.

The Continental Congress also named itself the provisional government of the thirteen colony-states: New Hampshire, Massachusetts, Connecticut, Rhode Island, New York, New Jersey, Pennsylvania, Delaware, Maryland, Virginia, North Carolina, South Carolina, and Georgia. The congress began acting without the approval of the British Parliament, forming an American postal service separate from the existing British one, issuing and borrowing money, and creating a navy and other armed forces. Seeing that the Continental Congress was the only assembly representing all the thirteen colonies, it also came down to the congressmen to decide how the colonies should proceed in the budding revolutionary war. The congress voted to remain defensive and focus the American military on the British forces in Boston.

However, before George Washington had the chance to follow the orders or even take command over the military, Gen. Thomas Gage began attempting to drive the colonial Americans out from Boston's oldest neighborhood of Charlestown. Small assaults would continue until June 17, 1775, when Americans would succeed in winning back Boston in the vicious Battle of Bunker Hill, which wiped out over 40 percent of the British troops involved. George Washington would assume command over the military a few weeks later, on July 3rd. By this time, more British forces had assembled in Boston, forcing him to focus his attention on containing the battles and holding the city. Over the following months, Washington would continue to defend the colonies as battles swept across Massachusetts and New York while also attempting to recruit men for his Continental Army, which was still quite small in comparison to the British forces.

Meanwhile, as battles raged on throughout many of the thirteen colonies, the Continental Congress continued to meet to discuss military strategy and their final demands. At the start of the Revolutionary War, the congress planned to remain a British colony, simply with more freedom. But by mid-1776, after over a year of battles, that no longer seemed like an option. First brought up by Richard Henry Lee of Virginia on July 2, 1776, the Continental Congress voted and finally resolved that "these United Colonies are, and of right ought to be, free and independent states." Two days later, on July 4th, which is now known as the United States of America's Independence Day, the Continental Congress officially declared independence from England. Throughout the rest of 1776, the colonies' battles for revolution continued, with both sides constantly losing and gaining superiority in the battle. As France and Britain had been in wars of their own only a few years previous in Canada, France decided to back the colonies in the Revolutionary War, which helped topple the scales in favor of the Americans.

The Battle of Yorktown

After a series of ups and downs for both the British and American troops, the battles finally entered Virginia for the second time throughout the Revolutionary War in May of 1781, in what would become known as the siege (or Battle) of Yorktown. After winning battles in North Carolina, General Lord Cornwallis, the British commander for the South, marched with his troops to Petersburg, Virginia, where they were to meet up with troops sent by another British commander stationed in the north, Sir Henry Clinton. Moving through Richmond and Williamsburg, Cornwallis led his troops to the coastal town of Yorktown, where he could maintain seaborne communication with British forces in the north.

While Cornwallis began setting up fortifications in Yorktown in July, George Washington ordered Marquis de Lafayette, a young Frenchman given command of many troops in Virginia, to block off any land routes Cornwallis' men could possibly use to escape Yorktown. Still stationed in New York with 2,500 troops, Washington was met by another French army general supporting the American revolutionary movement—Jean-Baptiste-Donatien de Vimeur (Comte de Rochambeau)—and his 4,000 French troops, who had just arrived from France. Towards the end of August, leaving a secure number of troops in New York to face any possible threats, Washington and Rochambeau's troops marched south towards Chesapeake Bay, where they joined with François Joseph Paul, Comte de Grasse, a French commander who was waiting with a fleet of ships and a few thousand French troops. Until that point, Comte de Grasse's naval army had been defending the sea to prevent Cornwallis' escape or further British reinforcements from the waterways. The combined Franco-American army boarded on Comte de Grasse's ships and continued by water south towards Virginia. After debarking in Williamsburg, the group joined Lafayette, who had successfully trapped Cornwallis in Yorktown thus far.

By the end of summer, the Franco-American troops had completely outnumbered the British forces in Yorktown. Although the English generals attempted to send more fleets to Virginia, all were stopped on the waterways by Comte de Grasse's stronger fleet of ships and promptly returned to New York, where the British military was stationed. With no way to get communication to the surrounded

Yorktown, Cornwallis had little idea as to why his reinforcements were delayed.

Throughout September and early October of 1781, the Franco-American troops patiently overwhelmed the British fortification, significantly outnumbering the British troops in men, guns, and position and gradually running down their food supply. In mid-October, the British forces finally managed to send out a fleet that could overwhelm the French defensive ships, but it would be too late, as on October 19, Cornwallis surrendered for the entire British army and thus ended the American Revolution. Overall, considering the bloodshed at some of the other battles, there were very few casualties suffered on either side in this decisive battle. That being said, there were gains and losses in other ways. The American army would capture around 8,000 British prisoners, over 200 guns, and—the largest win of all—unofficial independence over the colonies.

The American Revolution After the Battle of Yorktown

During the proceedings and the actual battle of Yorktown, the Continental Congress continued to meet with as many members as possible to arrange military decisions and future laws and acts for after the end of the revolution. Throughout the war, the congress wrote the Articles of Confederation, which would officially become the first Constitution of the United States of America in March of 1781 after being approved by all the colonies. Although at this time the US was united in war, the colonies, now known as states, operated more like independent nations. The somewhat loosely official Articles of Confederation would give the Continental Congress power over war measures (which they had already been governing) and foreign affairs, which had already been established, as well—the best examples being their alliance with France during the revolution and the power to regulate currency. Of course, while all this was written in the Articles of Confederation, and the congress was already performing much of the liberties that the Articles accorded them, they still had no official authority over the states, as they were, until the end of the Revolution, under the ownership of the British. The congress also had no way to actually enforce its laws, military measures, or financial requests from the states. States that still had a large British loyalist population had very little reason to give in to the congress' demands.

Following the end of the Battle at Yorktown, the war in America gradually dissipated. For the next few years, while peace treaties were being written and agreed upon, battles continued on the seas. Though America had fought Britain's fleets of ships during the earlier years of the American Revolutionary War, which officially was fought from Apr. 19, 1775, to Sep. 3, 1783, after forcing British forces to surrender in Yorktown, their involvement in naval battles was minute. Other than some American privateering, the war at sea that continued the American Revolutionary War for almost two years after the Battle at Yorktown was almost entirely fought between Britain and America's European allies, including France, Spain, and the Netherlands.

Throughout 1772, loyalists and troops slowly left the United States, the majority of which were now American patriots, in favor of England and Britain's newly -acquired colonies in Canada. On November 30, 1782, Britain and the previously British colonies of America signed preliminary peace agreements. Then, finally, on September 3, 1783, the two nations signed the Peace of Paris Agreement, which would put an official end to the American Revolutionary War. The United States would officially be considered an independent nation, spanning from the eastern coast (minus Florida, which had been ceded to Spain) to the western Mississippi River. Otherwise, the agreement stated that British loyalists or citizens remaining in the United States should be treated as American citizens, established the payment of outstanding debts that the United States would owe to Britain, and settled what usage Americans would have of Canadian fisheries, specifically in Newfoundland.

Following the signing of the Paris Peace Agreement, the final British forces that had remained stationed in New York left the United States of America and returned home to England. Following that symbolic action, George Washington triumphantly entered New York City to officially celebrate the win for the American forces. Thereafter, land action in America died out, though the war persisted in other theatres and on the high seas. Eventually, Clinton was replaced by Sir Guy Carleton. While the peace treaties were under consideration and afterward, Carleton evacuated thousands of loyalists from America, including many from Savannah on July 11, 1782, and others from Charleston on December 14. The last British forces finally left New York on November 25, 1783. In the few years following, the states would slowly rebuild their towns, economies, and political systems, all of which had been greatly altered by the war. The states began to construct their own systems for the first time in history, completely separate from British influence.

Chapter 8 – Post-Revolutionary Period and Virginia During and After the American Civil War (1783–1899)

Virginia's Role in Building the United States of America

In 1776, the capital of the United States had been moved from England's colonial capital in Virginia to the newly-formed nation's most populous city and the place where its first declared its independence—Philadelphia, Pennsylvania. Yet, despite the capital's location change, Virginia was still a massive player on the American political stage. During the American Revolution, Virginia had been the state largest both in territory and population, and it had contributed many of the greatest political players in early American history: George Washington, Thomas Jefferson, James Madison, James Monroe—four of America's founding fathers and four of the first five presidents, all hailing from Virginia. Another Virginian, Patrick Henry, was considered the "voice" of the American Revolution, as he wrote speeches to sway the American people in favor of freedom. One of his more notable quotes was: "Give me liberty, or give me death!" Some even consider Thomas Jefferson to be the pen (as he wrote the Declaration of Independence) and George Washington to be the sword (leading the Continental Army) of the revolution. In other words, to many historians, three Virginian natives helped lead the revolution and acquire the United States' independence from England.

As the Revolutionary War continued to rage on throughout the colonies, James Madison, Thomas Jefferson, and another Virginia-born politician, George Mason, worked to form the new government for the future United States of America. They determined that the American people should be entitled to inherent human rights (life and liberty) and that church and state must be separated from one another for the government to adequately protect the fundamental rights of its people. These concepts were accompanied by the beliefs that the role of government is to serve the people; citizens should have the right to vote for their government; citizens should have the right to a fair trial and due process of the law, freedom of speech and of the press, and religious expression; and standing armies are a threat to liberty. All were introduced by these three Virginians as they helped to form the Declaration of Rights in June of 1776, the Declaration of Independence in July of 1776, the Virginia Statute for Religious Freedom in 1786, the Constitution of the United States in 1786, and the first amendments to the Constitution in 1791.

Virginian men would also play critical roles in establishing the United States of America's legislative, executive, and judicial branches. James Madison, known as the Father of the Constitution, is credited with being the principal author of the United States Constitution and also led the debates on its rights. Three years after the creation of the original Constitution, James Madison would help draft some of America's most fundamental laws as he assumed the role of leader of the House of Representatives. In 1789, George Washington would be named the first president of the United States. Considering he had led the military forces in the American Revolution, he was respected and trusted by American patriots, making it easy to lead the newly-formed nation in its early years. During his term as president, Washington would construct new courts, agencies, foreign affairs relationships, and domestic legislation, essentially laying the building blocks of modern-day America. Finally, there's John Marshall, who is credited with building America's independent federal judiciary and its central government. He helped to establish fundamental American rights, such as the Supreme Court's power to overrule legislative legal action and unconstitutional executive and state laws. Marshall would serve as chief justice of the United States between 1801 and 1835.

Virginia in the Late 18th to Early 19th Century

Despite Virginia's significant contribution to building the United States in its budding years, following the American Revolution, the state itself was suffering. Although Virginia would continue to grow alongside the other states, it could not keep up with its rapidly developing neighbors. Its main pitfall, ironically, was its original shining blessing—the tobacco crop. Tobacco had been the crux of Virginia's economy since its introduction to Virginia by John Rolfe in the early 1600s. Considering the incredible demand for Virginia's unique strain of tobacco, farmers overplanted the crop to meet European requests, and by the late 18th century, they were starting to feel the consequences. At this time, concepts of the necessity of crop rotation and fertilizer were unknown to farmers (except perhaps to the Native Americans, who had better understanding of the land). By 1800, the land in the Tidewater and Piedmont regions was so gullied and stripped of nutrients that little could grow at all. Nothing grown in the overused fields of Virginia could meet the quality of seasons past or that of other states. It was said that the soil was so depleted and overused that, when it rained in Virginia, so much soil would run off into the waterways that it looked like rivers of blood. It was not just the tobacco industry that was suffering, either. Essentially all farming in Virginia suffered, and throughout the first few decades of the 19th century, land values in Virginia plummeted by more than one hundred million dollars.

After the difficult years of the American Revolutionary War and the inability to grow its most profitable crop, Virginia was impoverished. Considering that the poor growing seasons were not going to change anytime soon and Virginia's economy was almost entirely based on tobacco farming, by the end of the millennium, it became obvious to many Virginians that their state could not offer them the economic opportunities necessary for growth, let alone upward momentum in society. Before long, Virginians began migrating elsewhere. The state that had once been the most populated state is estimated to have lost over one million people between the American Revolution and the Civil War. Furthermore, the original prestige associated with Virginia was gone, as wealthy citizens emigrated and Virginians struggled to make ends meet in its dying economy. Though America was being built by politically influential Virginians, few of them would actually remain in their birth state.

America's Expansion and Westward Spread

Virginia's mass emigration was extremely well-timed with America's expansion, which opened up many possibilities for Virginians looking to build wealth elsewhere. America would acquire many westward states in the first years following its official independence, when growth was the main priority. During the French Revolution, the United States would re-involve itself with its old ally, but this time as a mostly neutral party as the second and the third US presidents, Thomas Jefferson and James Madison, attempted to remain afloat during the Napoleonic Wars. England and France's involvement in the Napoleonic Wars would prove to be both positive and negative to America, as the newly-developed United States would suffer without its main trade partners whose economies were strained. Still, the United States managed to benefit, as France's suffering economy allowed it to purchase Louisiana.

In 1804, America would continue to expand as Thomas Jefferson designated Meriwether Lewis with the responsibility of exploring west of the current states. Lewis would enlist mapmaker William Clark, and over the course of two years, the two would discover land spreading from just west of the current states all the way to the Pacific Ocean. This discovery would later lead to Thomas Jefferson's purchase of Louisiana, which had almost been returned to France. By the end of the first quarter of the 19th century, the United States of America's territory would almost double in size. As all the land outside of Louisiana (which had been partially colonized by France) was completely undeveloped, the newly-acquired lands had totally open economies—another attractive reason for Virginians to leave their home state. Virginian natives would quickly rise to leadership in the new states. For example, John Sevier would become the first governor of Tennessee in 1796, the year it achieved statehood. Henry Clay, who would become a prominent politician in Kentucky in the early 19th century, is another example of the many Virginians who would fortunately arrive in the newly-acquired states just as they were developing their politics, economy, and culture.

Positive Repercussions of Virginia's Mass Emigration

Of course, Virginia's soil depletion, loss of its most profitable crop, and mass emigration did not have an entirely positive impact on a state that was already struggling due to the American Revolutionary War. That being said, there were some positive ramifications among the negative. For more than two centuries, Virginia's entire economy was based on one crop, and of course, when that crop began to fail, its economy began to fail. While that system may have worked when Virginia was a barely-developed colony focusing on survival, Virginia would need to develop other industries to compete with other American states. In 1804, Virginia would develop its own state-chartered banks that could offer retail and commercial loans and services to Virginians attempting to build up businesses. Over the next few years, Virginia would undergo massive territorial development as it constructed roads, canals, railroads, and homes. These endeavors not only offered jobs to Virginians but also aided in making the most underdeveloped state more livable and attractive to immigrants and potential emigrants. By the mid-19th century, Virginia had founded many more public schools and colleges, which would help educate Virginia's population, attract students from other states, and retain wealthy families who wished to educate their children.

Over the first half of the 19th century, Virginia would build up manufacturing industries (essentially, an economy less dependent on farming), as the soil would not be ready for mass agriculture, specifically single-crop farming, for many more years. With the help of the chartered banks, Virginians began opening large factories all over the state, though most were centered in Richmond, which was rapidly becoming one of the manufacturing hubs of America. Before long, Virginia would begin trading directly with other states all over the United States, as well as countries in South America and Europe, which would help revive its economy. By 1860, Virginia was manufacturing in higher quantities than any other southern state.

To make matters better, wealthy Virginian planters whose families had remained in the state, such as Edmund Ruffin, were slowly developing more advanced methods of agriculture with the invention of fertilizers and theories of crop rotation. This would allow farming to slowly make its way back into the Virginian economy. However, despite the upward momentum, it would be many more decades before Virginia's economy actually repaired itself from the damage done by mass tobacco farming. It would not be until the 20th century that the state would actually be able to compare or compete with other American states, which had also been growing at rapid speeds but without the difficult setbacks Virginia had to face.

Unlike the earlier history of Virginia in which many of its citizens were self-made millionaires, in the 19th century, the United States government would be the largest employer in Virginia as the state constructed its economy and infrastructures. Riches in Virginia in the

19th century were mostly passed down through families. If you were unfortunate enough not to be born or married into a wealthy family, you were likely working for the government at a livable but un-extravagant wage, making it difficult to achieve upward momentum. While its history, families, and culture would remain steadfast, Virginia was developing rapidly. The mostly rural territory transformed into a more urban and cosmopolitan area centered on large-scale manufacturing.

Overall, Virginia's economic struggles would be necessary to rebuild an economy that had a fundamental flaw from the very beginning. The only real issue was that it would face its financial difficulties as other states were growing rapidly instead of before, when it had the advantage of being America's first colony. Gradually, tobacco farming would return to Virginia, although it would not be the single source of the state's income as it had been before. By the mid-1800s, Virginia would once again become an epicenter of tobacco, as Richmond became the world's tobacco production hub.

Other than the rebuilding of Virginia's economy, there would be other major benefits to its mass emigration in the post-revolutionary period. Since so many Virginians were leaving the state, those who remained felt it was their duty to preserve Virginia's glorious history. By 1831, the state had formed the Virginia Historical Society; its creation is a direct repercussion of mass emigration in Virginia. As mentioned previously, Virginia's mass emigration led Virginians to build wealth, social connections, and influence elsewhere in America. With that expansion of people came the expansion of Virginia's culture. Though Virginia had joined and led the American Revolution and helped to establish the beliefs, laws, politics, government, and culture of the United States, every state had certainly developed its own unique culture by this point. Virginia had quite a head start in comparison to some of the states that were just being formed at the end of the 18th century and the beginning of the 19th century.

Other than the Native American tribes with their own unique cultures, there was no established culture among the settlers in these newly-formed states. Immigrants who arrived in these new settlements brought with them their own state's culture. As Virginia had the largest rates of emigration among the states, it was Virginia's culture that would spread the most through the newly-forming states, specifically those in the South. Before long, Virginia's unique culture, laws, beliefs, political ideas, architecture, social concepts, and labor systems had spread westward, mostly throughout the southern states. One of the more notable concepts that spread from Virginia to other American states was that of slavery.

Slavery in Virginia and Other Southern States

Slavery in Virginia dates back to 1619, when the first slaves arrived in America. Over the course of the 17th century, owning slaves wove itself into the fundamental fabric of Virginia. By the beginning of the 18th century, Virginians would see owning slaves as a display of wealth, just as owning a large home or designer clothes would be seen today. Before long, owning slaves became a fundamental right in Virginia, as introduced in the Slave Codes of 1705. During the pre-revolutionary period, tobacco farmers built their empires on the backs of slaves, as one could simply not produce as much product at so little cost by paying employees livable wages.

However, as times grew tougher and the economy suffered during the Revolutionary War, many slave owners let go of their slaves. This likely had less to do with being against the principle of slavery and more to do with cutting the budget when product demand was low and men were busy at war. Among the men who freed some or all of their slaves were Virginia natives George Washington and Thomas Jefferson. Although Jefferson only freed some of his slaves, he joined the northern states in criticizing slave ownership and eventually aided in abolishing the African slave trade in Virginia in 1778. Yet, despite having abolished slavery in Virginia, Virginians continued to own slaves openly and proudly as they had before.

Meanwhile, as Virginians rapidly emigrated and moved to other (mostly neighboring, southern) states, the state's beliefs about slave ownership and the demand for slaves spread, as well. Demand for slaves grew especially quickly in southern states as cotton clothing gained popularity and the rapid demand for cotton farming skyrocketed. However, as Mississippi, Alabama, Georgia, Arkansas, Texas, and Louisiana's cotton industries and demand for slaves boomed, Virginia's land, agricultural production, and requirement for slaves were rapidly declining. In the early 19th century, many wealthy families remaining in Virginia began selling a majority of their slaves as quickly as possible as the prices for slaves tanked in Virginia. By the end of the first quarter of the 19th century, slaves in Virginia were being sold for around a third (or in some cases, even a fourth) of the price of slaves in other states as slave owners flooded the slave market and essentially deflated the worth of their slaves.

While at first this was viewed negatively, as the demand for slaves gradually skyrocketed in nearby states, the decreased price of slaves in Virginia would become somewhat of a blessing for its slave owners. Slave owners began sending hundreds of thousands of slaves to New Orleans and selling slaves to people willing to resell them in New Orleans, where slaves could be bought for triple the price or more. Before long, a significant slave market had developed in Virginia—specifically in Richmond, where nearly thirty slave auction houses had sprung up within only a decade or so. By the mid-19th century, Richmond became the second slave-trading center in America, after New Orleans, whose slave markets were older and more centralized among the other slave-owning states. Finally, by the 1830s, as the manufacturing and farming industries began forming, owning slaves once again became commonplace among Virginians.

The booming slave trade was beneficial to the wealthy who sold and bought slaves, the employees who ran markets and transported the slaves, and the state and federal governments whose economies boomed. It was beneficial to almost all—except for, of course, the slaves themselves. The wealthy of Virginia and other states had slaves who not only performed agricultural and manufacturing labor jobs but also worked directly for the wealthy—cooking and serving their meals, raising their children, and cleaning their homes. Those with specific skills, such as blacksmithing, were no better off and were forced to work in unthinkable conditions for their slave owners.

Yet, despite how slavery was so intrinsically tied to the wealthy culture in the South, slave owners were generally afraid of possible revolts and resistance movements. Management of slaves was commonly discussed among the wealthy, who worked together to ensure they remained in power. After generations of owning slaves, slave owners determined strict rules and conduct systems that would prevent resistance: some positive incentives, intense physical punishment, making examples out of those who misbehaved (or tried to escape), and, in most cases, prohibiting slaves from leaving the grounds, learning to read, or meeting with other slaves. Laws were even put in place in Virginia to severely punish white Virginians who attempted to help slaves, whether it be something as small as teaching them to read or as large as helping them escape. Even those who visited Virginia from other slave-owning states often found Virginia's practices to be extreme or downright appalling.

Despite the severity of the methods, Virginia's practices were certainly nowhere near foolproof. Conditions for enslaved Virginians' lives were often so horrendous that slaves did not care what punishment they endured—even death would be better than remaining slaves. Many slave owners experienced highly organized rebellions and (in more extreme cases) attempted escapes, which usually ended poorly for both sides but worse for the slaves. Almost every home in Virginia would experience some form of resistance, but most acts of resistance were small, such as stealing, working slower than possible, or breaking labor tools.

In the earlier years of slavery, Virginian slave owners tended to be significantly less strict than in the years following the 1830s, though they were still extremely cruel to their slaves. During those early years, Virginian slaves developed their own communities, culture, music, folklore, religion, food traditions, and more. Even the strictest slave owners usually allowed slaves to take Sunday off from work, as they would work more efficiently with a rest day. On these Sundays, the slaves would engage with their family and friends, attend church, and tend to their own agricultural projects if they were allowed to have any. It was likely these habits, along with the art forms created during this time, that enabled enslaved individuals to survive and keep the will to live through even the cruelest circumstances. Through these communications with family and friends, usually at church, the Black community discussed their circumstances, and those willing to take risks planned acts of resistance and rebellions.

While there were many notable rebellions in Virginia, one of the more famous was the Nat Turner Revolt, named for an enslaved African American preacher who, on August 21, 1831, led a group of hundreds of fellow slaves in a rebellion against slavery in Virginia. The groups of slaves killed fifty-eight white slave owners and their families, and in response, almost 200 African Americans involved in the rebellion would lose their lives, as well. Close to forty more people would also die trying to protect members of both sides during the event and in smaller violent resistance movements. After the event, Nat Turner and nineteen of his co-conspirators would be tried and executed by the state of Virginia. In the end, the Nat Turner Revolt would become known as the bloodiest slave revolt in all of American history. Many credit this violent series of events in 1831 with worsening the already incredibly strict, horrendous conditions of slaves in Virginia, as laws prohibiting the education, movement, and assembly of enslaved people were passed as a response to the revolt.

Although Nat Turner's Revolt was unsuccessful for the conspirators and many of the slaves involved, it was not an altogether failure, either, as it fueled the conversation about slavery throughout the nation. In Virginia was a small group that promoted the abolition of slavery, and that group got even smaller after the Nat Turner Revolt. Virginia framed it as an obvious sign of African Americans' violent characteristics and explained that future revolts could be avoided if fewer liberties were given to the enslaved communities. However, the conversation was not entirely one-sided, and the Virginian government was forced to consider the fate of slavery in the state due to the outcry from antislavery proponents. In the 1831–1832 session, the Virginia General Assembly would vote to maintain slavery. However, the voting itself was quite a big deal, as this would be the first and only time any slave state would consider (let alone vote on) ending slavery until they would be forced to during the Civil War. The revolt would also help fuel the case for the abolition of slavery in other (mostly northern) states, some of which had already put an end to slave-owning and were hoping to do so in the rest of America, as well.

The Lead Up to the Civil War

During the early years of the 19th century, the northern states of America's economy rapidly grew and, before long, blew past struggling Virginia and other newly-formed southern states. In the South, the economy was almost entirely dependent on plantation farming (with the exception of Virginia, of course). By contrast, in the northern states, the economy was much more diversified and debatably more modernized. Banking, insurance, books, and media-spreading sources such as the newspaper took massive roles in the economy. Diversification of the economy was necessary because the northern states simply did not have as long of a growing season as southern states did, making it hard to compete economically with farming alone. While there was, of course, farming and some slave labor in the North, slave labor was much less necessary. As the income of most was not dependent on it, slave labor became less of a priority to most civilians. As slave labor became less necessary, more African Americans became free and played a part in society.

Before long, with no massive need for slaves to advance the economy, the question of the morality of owning slaves came to the forefront of society in the North. The first state to actually abolish slavery would be Pennsylvania, which made owning slaves illegal as early as 1780. The state was quickly followed by many other northern states who shared similar principles that had been spread and debated in schools, books, newspapers, and magazines. While the northern states and Virginia invested money in factories and railroads, most of the southern states invested their money in land and slaves. Diversification and modernization would, of course, prove to be useful later on, but in the early 19th century, they were quite unnecessary in the South, which had long growing seasons, low production costs, entirely free labor, and incredible demand for their products—most notably, cotton. By 1860, the majority of America's richest families were located in the South, and the southern states had more than twice the per capita wealth of the northern states.

Overall, it was almost as if the North and South were operating as different countries with completely different morals, economies, political systems, and cultures. While this system of operating separately worked for some time, tensions were growing between the North and South. As the country continued to acquire and induct new states and territories, including Missouri, California, and Texas, debates rose as to whether these new states should allow slavery or abolish slavery. In 1848, at the end of the Mexican-American War, when the United States would acquire much of its southwestern territory (around 500,000 square miles of land), the conversation was accelerated as each new state government debated slavery.

By the 1850s, the northern states could not stand idle any longer and felt that America—a civilized, modernized nation—should not be represented by something that was so outdated and morally wrong.

They began calling for the official abolishment of slavery throughout all the United States, not just the northern states. On the other hand, the southern states were not fighting for the morality of the institution. Contrary to what some may believe, not all southerners felt it was morally right to own slaves. In the South, slaves were seen as a tool, just as machinery is seen today. It was a way to advance production, saving money and time. Therefore, when it came time to defend owning slaves, the southern states were not defending the moral practice of owning slaves but the economic and political rights of owning slaves. The southern states felt the northern states—who had diversified economies less dependent on farming and therefore less dependent on slaves—were attempting to oppressively assert authority over the South, take away its main sources of income, and worst of all, take away a right that its citizens then believed to be fundamental. As slave-owning had been so fundamentally intertwined with social, political, and economic systems since the creation of Virginia and the other southern states' economies, it came as no surprise that they felt so strongly about not losing that right.

The southern states also felt strongly about bringing slavery into the newly-acquired American states, which would allow them to expand their plantations into the new territories and trade slaves to new markets. Throughout the 1850s, tensions would continue to rise between the North and the South as they became increasingly polarized on the issues surrounding slavery. By the 1860 presidential election, the topic of the right to own slaves was a fundamental component to each runner's campaign: the Republicans in favor of abolishing slavery and the Democrats the opposite. After months of tense election campaigns, on November 6, 1860, Republican candidate Abraham Lincoln would be elected as the 19th president of the United States. Lincoln won the election with no favorable ballots from any of the eleven future Confederate states except for Virginia, where only a little over one percent of the votes were for Lincoln— almost all of these located in what would eventually become West Virginia. Lincoln's victory was a symbol that Virginia and the other southern states had lost majority power. Although Virginia had helped build the US government system and write its constitution, Virginia and the other slave-owning states would decide to secede from the United States of America.

The American Civil War

Virginia was not the first state to leave the Union following Lincoln's election. It was preceded by seven states that had seceded in 1860: South Carolina, Mississippi, Florida, Alabama, Georgia, Louisiana, and Texas. The separate states attempted to form a new nation, known as the Confederacy, which would have its own government, laws, and command of all within its territory. While the Confederacy claimed all the US forts and arsenals on its land, two government forts in Confederate territory remained under Union government control: Fort Pickens, Florida, and Fort Sumter in Charleston, South Carolina. Although they held no real strategic benefit, the Confederacy demanded both remaining forts be evacuated and handed over to them, as they represented a symbol of their independence and influence.

When President Lincoln was finally sworn into office to begin his term in March of the following year, he was greeted with the hard decision of what to do about the Confederacy's demands before he could even tackle the issue of slavery or any other of his campaign promises. Not wanting to recognize the legitimacy of the union, Lincoln decided it would be best to defend the forts and attempted to send supplies and relief expeditions to both Fort Pickens and Fort Sumter. Before anything arrived at either of the forts, the Confederacy demanded that both forts (most immediately Fort Sumter, which was closer to the Union's territory and would therefore receive the supplies/defense faster) be evacuated immediately. Otherwise, there would be war. Lincoln refused, and on April 12, 1861, the Confederacy, led by P.G.T. Beauregard, began attacking Fort Sumter. After a day and a half of battle, the outnumbered Union soldiers, led by Maj. Robert Anderson, were forced to surrender and officially hand Fort Sumter over to the Confederacy.

The Battle of Fort Sumter would not only officially kick off the American Civil War but also force the other states to pick a side more rapidly than they had anticipated. While the states had already been debating the issue, within a few days after the battle, they began speeding up voting on whether to remain in the Union or join the Confederacy. In the early months of 1861, Virginia would hold its own convention to debate the issue. While Virginia had hoped to keep the Union intact (after all, there were a number of Union supporters in Virginia, almost entirely concentrated in present-day West Virginia), following Lincoln's decision to defend the forts on Confederate land, the state would vote in favor of succession on April 4, 1861.

Though the official date of Virginia's secession is somewhat debated since it held multiple votes and at one point temporarily joined the Confederacy, Virginia had officially succeeded from the United States of America by the beginning of the summer of 1861. It would be followed by Arkansas, Tennessee, and North Carolina. As Virginia was strategically important to the Confederacy, the capital of the Confederacy was moved from Montgomery, Alabama to Richmond, Virginia shortly after Virginia joined. By the time of the Civil War, Virginia had become the industrial center of the South, and its proximity to the Union would make it easier to secure other states to join the Confederacy and to engage in battles with the northern states.

Meanwhile, both the Union and the Confederacy began preparing for war by investing money in supplies, manufacturing weapons, building up armies, and attempting to sway undecided states. By the end of 1861, each side had built a military with its own advantages and disadvantages. The Union outnumbered the Confederacy by twelve states and around twelve million people. Of the nine million people in the South, almost half were actually slaves. The Union states also had more manufacturing plants, railroads, arms production, funding, manpower, and of course, a more established army. Yet, the Confederacy had the advantage of interior lines. In other words, it had a smaller area to defend and less distance to travel to fight, meaning travel would be less inconvenient, exhausting, and expensive. Soldiers in the South also tended to be more passionate about the cause. Defending one's rights (in this case, the right to own slaves) was a southern institution, and the Confederacy did not need to call for military conscription, as the Union was forced to.

Throughout the Civil War, which raged from the Battle of Fort Sumter in 1861 until April 9th, 1865, Virginia would host more battles than any other state in America. This comes as no surprise considering its proximity to the Union states and its divided population. In fact, the first major land battle in the Civil War is considered to have been the First Battle of Bull Run. Until that battle, the Union—knowing of their many advantages over the Confederacy—believed the Civil War would be an easy victory, and Lincoln ordered forces to march straight into Richmond to take down the Confederate forces in their capital and put a decisive end to the war. Yet, on July 21, 1861, the Union forces, led by Brigadier General Irvin McDowell, were intercepted by Confederate forces led by P.G.T. Beauregard near Manassas Junction, Virginia. The battle was expected to be so easy for the Union forces that civilians from Washington had actually arrived at the battlefield with their families and picnics to watch the swift defeat of the Confederacy. However, that would not be the case. With incredible feats of military strategy, the Confederacy managed to defeat the more organized Union troops and send them retreating back to Washington.

After the First Battle of Bull Run, Abraham Lincoln and the Union states were forced to reconsider their opinion of the Confederacy, which they had not expected to be a threat at all. This battle was not so different from many of the battles won by the Confederacy: the Union underestimated the disadvantaged troops; the Confederate leaders, at quite a disadvantage, relied on incredible military strategy and prowess to defeat the Union.

But the First Battle of Bull Run filled the southern states with a sense of false hope and overconfidence. Even though they had won, the Confederate troops were overall less organized than the Union's. The war would continue as such, with battles won and lost by both sides and the advantage in the war constantly changing. Many more battles would be fought in Virginia, most notably the Second Battle of Bull Run, the Seven Days Battles in Richmond, the Battle of Fredericksburg in 1862, Chancellorsville in 1863, and the Wilderness to Petersburg Campaign (Battle of the Wilderness) in 1864–65. Many of the most decisive battles in the war would be fought in Virginia, and the state would provide some of the most revolutionary and important military strategists in American history, including Confederate General Stonewall Jackson and commanding General Robert E. Lee. However, despite the incredible military strategy and strong effort put forth by the Confederate states, their disadvantages would cause them to gradually lose the war. In April of 1865, Confederate General Robert E. Lee surrendered to the Union military in the Battle of Appomattox Court House in Virginia, officially putting an end to the American Civil War.

Virginia's Reconstruction Post-Civil War

The American Civil War had many effects on Virginia, none more obvious than the literal splitting of the state, as the massive state of Virginia was separated into two in 1863. The new state, which was made up of one-third of Virginia's original territory, would become known as West Virginia. Although the loss of one third of Virginia's territory was quite a blow to the state, Virginia had little time to determine the full effects of the division, as the war was still raging on at that time. By the end of the war, Virginia, which had hosted a majority of the battlegrounds, was in ruins. The state's farms, railroads, bridges, and many of its buildings were destroyed. To make matters worse, Virginia's money, which had been converted into

Confederate currency during the Civil War, had no value in the Union. Its banks were promptly closed, and its economy was even worse off than in usual postwar scenarios. The Union government at the time had many of its own issues to debate—namely, how to house, feed, and employ all of the now free slaves—and decided to allow the Confederate states the chance to "reconstruct" their own governments before they rejoined the United States Union.

However, just because Virginia had lost the war did not mean it had changed its mind about the original conflict. Virginia's post-war government continued to restrict the rights of slaves and essentially keep their former laws, beliefs, and politicians in place, as was the case in most of the other previously Confederate states. However, this did not last long. By 1867, Congress had put the entire South under military rule and quickly established laws that allowed African American men the right to vote. The state of Virginia pledged to begin rebuilding its railroads and establish new schools, and in 1870, the state was readmitted to the Union. A new constitution that reformed much of Virginia's systems, notably the education and tax systems, was agreed upon that same year.

For a few years in the 1870s, Virginia appeared to be advancing towards a more Republican political atmosphere, as many African Americans ran for office in elections and Republicans from northern states began arriving in Virginia looking for work. As complete reconstruction of the state was necessary, ideologies were of little debate, and the Virginians instead focused on fixing the infrastructure and economy that had been damaged during the war. The government introduced free food, medical care, and schooling for citizens and even began renting land to help farmers reestablish the state's farming industry.

However, once rebuilding was over, the political shift did not follow through, and by the end of the 1870s, Virginia began returning to its previously Democratic ideologies. Before long, statues of Confederate leaders were being put up all over towns, and citizens pledged allegiance to the old institutions of Virginia even more rigorously than before. The Democratic Party in Virginia was revived in 1883, and before long, the Jim Crow Laws, which enforced segregation of the races, were introduced. When back in government, the Democratic Party of Virginia controversially readjusted its debt and successfully demanded that West Virginia help cover a third.

By 1937, Virginia would have fully paid off its debts, but until then, the economy suffered as it slowly rebuilt. Virginia's economy in the late 19th century and early 20th century would be almost entirely focused on rebuilding the railroads and agriculture, as it once again returned to its roots of tobacco farming. With the reconstruction of the railroads, Virginia was able to slowly expand its industrial range, and manufacturing factories for the timber, coal, cigarette, and textile industries quickly emerged. Despite its economic issues and the slow rate at which rural Virginia would develop, urban Virginia would modernize quickly at the end of the 19th century, introducing electricity into the major cities. Richmond even became the site of the world's first large-scale streetcar system.

Chapter 9 – Virginia in the 20th Century (1900–2000)

It did not take long after the post-Civil War reconstruction before Virginia found itself returning to its original government, ideologies, and economy. In 1902, Virginia adopted a new constitution with revisions that truly only benefited wealthy and influential Virginians. Examples of these newly-adjusted measures include a literacy test and a poll tax for voters. This would, of course, exclude almost all African American citizens, who had not been allowed to learn how to read until after the Civil War, as well as poor citizens of all races who could not pay the required poll tax to vote.

Since Virginia had been separated from the Republican, Union-supporting West Virginia and almost all African Americans in Virginia were Republican (as that was the party that actually accorded them rights), these new laws helped ensure the Democratic Party's supremacy in the state. For almost 100 years (between 1874 and 1970), Virginia's governor would be Democratic—except for four years where the governor was essentially a variation of a Democrat called a Readjuster. During this time, Virginian senators, including Thomas S. Martin and Harry F. Byrd, enforced Democratic laws such as low taxes, white supremacy, and forced segregation that kept Black

Virginians from moving upward in society. The situation was better, but not much better, for non-wealthy and white female Virginians. In the northern states, women's suffrage movements were quickly advancing women's rights, some states having allowed women to vote as early as the mid-19th century. However, in Virginia, women's rights movements were delayed by a few decades and would not really begin until the 1910s. Although Virginia would vote against it, in 1920, the United States of America would ratify the 19th Amendment, which would allow white women to vote even in Virginia. That being said, Virginia would not officially ratify that legislation until 1952.

Another aspect of Virginia's culture that was completely restored after the Civil War was tobacco farming, as a new demand for pipes, cigars, and eventually cigarettes skyrocketed postwar. Virginia once again became the world's tobacco-growing hub, and its capital city, Richmond, became the world's cigarette capital. By the turn of the millennium, half of both Richmond and Petersburg's workforces were in the tobacco industry. By 1910, Virginia would have over 7,000 brands of smoking tobacco, 2,000 brands of cigarettes, cigarros, and cheroots, and 12,000 brands of plug, twist, and fine-cut chewing tobacco, manufacturing more alternatives than anywhere else in the world. Of course, competition would eventually force many brands to close or merge to survive, and over the decades, only a few pertinent ones would remain.

World War I

World War I also affected Virginia. Although 3,700 Virginians would lose their lives, the Great War affected the state in mostly positive ways. Over 100,000 Virginians served in World War I, forcing Virginia's women to take over positions in the workforce, which, as noted, would inspire the commencement of the women's suffrage movements in Virginia. Virginia's manufacturing industries would also be of great need during the war, and the state's navy yards and weapon-building factories would expand, contributing much-needed funds to the still-recovering economy. As the state's financial situation improved, business owners and local governments were able to invest more into agriculture. Before long, farming diversified, adding more major crops than just tobacco. In the years following the First World War, Virginia would also receive a boom of tourists, which would help build the budding tourism enterprise. To compensate, business owners quickly established hotels and tourist attractions, all of which would also aid in rebuilding the state's economy. The most important impact of World War I was likely the development of Virginia's military industry, which would become extremely necessary in the coming years.

The Great Depression

While the Great Depression was not easy on Virginia, as its agricultural and manufacturing industries suffered, it was certainly less severe than in other states. Virginia had fewer financial struggles than much of the rest of America, so the state had money that other states could just not afford to spend during the difficult times, and the government invested much of its money into military purposes. By the beginning of the 1940s, Virginia had established a state defense system—the very first one in the country.

World War II

World War II would put an end to the country's Great Depression, helping the economies of all the states—Virginia's more than others. The Second World War demanded mass manufacturing, which Virginia's factories could supply, and put into use Virginia's military development in earlier decades. Virginia would become the shipping location for over a million soldiers during World War II and the necessary training location of tens of thousands. By the end of World War II, Virginia's financial struggles, which dated back to the Revolutionary period, were finally resolved. Throughout the Second World War, Virginia's role as the heart of America's military branch was established. In 1941, the Pentagon would be constructed, and in 1947, the CIA was formed, both of which are still located in the state of Virginia.

Post World War II

When the Second World War ended in 1945, there was no doubt that the world was a better place. The same went for Virginia, which had benefited massively over the course of the conflict. Its high employment rate would continue after the war, as would the state's economic success, which after almost two decades of difficulties, was a much-needed change of pace. This gave Virginia's government and citizens time to focus on the internal social issues that were unable to be addressed while restoring the economy was the top priority. When the thousands of African American soldiers who fought in World War II, a war in part against cruel racial discrimination, returned home to Virginia, they were treated with the same intense racial discrimination as before. The battle of the races in Virginia would continue for years, and finally, in the 1950s, the state would begin to take steps towards desegregation.

In 1951, a sixteen-year-old student named Barbara Rose Johns led a walk-out protest in her segregated school in Virginia, which inspired a serious investigation and a series of debates on the constitutionality of segregated schools. By 1954, the United States Supreme Court would decide that segregated schools were no longer constitutional. Yet, despite the American government's decision, Virginia stubbornly closed schools that attempted to integrate—including in Barbara Johns' home of Prince Edward County, where schools that were ordered to integrate would remain closed for more than five years despite protests, forcing Black students to look elsewhere for schooling.

Finally, in the late 1960s, after the death of Harry F. Byrd, a staunch supporter of segregation, segregation would finally come to an end. Integrated schools in Virginia would finally open, and African Americans were also given the right to vote. Despite Virginia's delays in ending segregation and the continued difficulties for the African American population after the 1960s, Virginia would become the first state to elect an African American governor when L. Douglas Wilder was chosen to represent the state in 1989.

Chapter 10 – Present Day Virginia (2000–Today)

Considering that Virginia became the military hub of America, it would come as no surprise that the influx of foreign wars that went on over the latter half of the 20th century and the beginning of the 21st century was beneficial to the state's government, economy, and growth. In the past fifty years or so, Virginia has grown exponentially, especially around the Washington, D.C. border, Richmond, and Hampton Roads areas, where the government, manufacturing, technological, and military infrastructures are mostly located. Booms in those industries created an influx of jobs and people, forcing Virginia's metropolitan areas to sprawl out into easily commutable suburbs. In the years following the Second World War, Virginia's economy essentially transformed into an incredibly affluent one. As is typical in states with high per capita incomes, Virginia has invested heavily in education and has a relatively highly educated population, especially in comparison to other southern states. In the 21st century, the largest industry is not tobacco farming but the government, followed by agriculture.

Despite the mass emigration from Virginia that occurred after the Revolutionary War and all the hardships that befell the state's economy, Virginians have remained a proud population that still hold strongly to their heritage and beliefs. While this is the attitude that has formed some of America's greatest presidents, military leaders, and most influential people, it is also an attitude that has caused the state to attract negative attention from the other states. Some notable cases of this were in the debates on same-sex marriage and on abortion, both of which are now legal in the state. As politics changed, the ideologies of the Democratic Party eventually transitioned into the current Republican Party. Yet, Virginia, unlike its fellow past Confederate states, is not an entirely Republican state but a split state. For many years, Virginia was a swing state in the election, meaning it was generally unpredictable, changing which party it would vote for from year to year. Yet, in the past decade, it seems Virginia is transitioning to a majority Democratic state, likely because of the large urban cities, which tend to be more Democratic than the rest of the country.

Conclusion

Virginia is an incredibly complex US state that developed its own unique and rich culture, ideologies, economy, and political system separate from its colonizing country of England early on. Because of this, it has been home to some of the most revolutionary thinkers, political figures, military leaders, and battlegrounds. However, its complex ideologies and systems have also placed the state on the wrong side of history in many cases, especially in the American Civil War, in which it found itself fighting for the Confederates and home to the capital of the Confederacy. Although it is easy for current Democrats or those located in the North to look down on Virginia for its past and even current beliefs, its history and development completely explain its people's ideologies.

Part of this explanation can be found in the reality that much of Virginia's early culture surrounded the farming of tobacco. Virginia became essentially a single-crop economy and, unlike the northern states that could not depend on farming due to a reduced growing season, tobacco farming became the crux of the state. Much like other rural states, slavery was in many ways the backbone of the state's economy. When northern states—which had developed economies less reliant on farming and therefore less reliant on slavery—demanded the abolishment of slavery, Virginia felt that its ideologies were at risk and its economy and freedom were being stripped away. This inevitably encouraged the state to join the Confederate States, whose cultures were also intertwined with slavery from their creation.

Despite its involvement in the Civil War and the difficult years towards social reformation in the post-war years, the state would eventually develop an economy without the need for slaves and without depending so entirely on tobacco. Nowadays, Virginia is quite a divided state, likely due to the fact that its economy is split between government jobs and farming jobs.

Much of Virginia's population, especially those who have generations of families who have remained rooted in Virginia, are quite proud of Virginia's heritage and history. Virginia is known to be the state with the most remaining memorials to the Confederacy in the US, and in the more rural areas, it does not seem that those monuments are going anywhere. However, with the increase of national protests against perceived symbols of racism, often followed by the removal of—and, in more extreme cases, destruction of— historic statues, the peacefulness of Virginia's future is somewhat uncertain. In Richmond, where statues of Confederate statues still stand, there is constant debate as to the morality of keeping memorials to these military leaders who find themselves on the wrong side of history. It would seem that in the coming years the currently Democratic government of Virginia will continue to remove statues and memorials.

While it may seem hard to understand why anyone would want to keep statues of figures that are considered racists today, it is important to keep in mind that Virginia's citizens are proud of their heritage and that the Confederate leaders that they celebrate were impressive leaders, nonetheless, whose strategy and intelligence are still taught and spoken about in schools today.

Today, Democratic Virginians and Republican Virginians, who respectively do not understand the state's offensive history and celebrate its rich legacy, live in one territory, divided. And, if the occurrences in the United States today bear any testimony to the future, Virginia will only continue to divide as each side's ideologies continue to clash with one another.

Here's another book by Captivating History that you might like

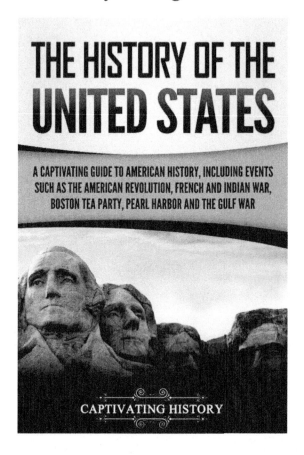

Free Bonus from Captivating History (Available for a Limited time)

Hi History Lovers!

Now you have a chance to join our exclusive history list so you can get your first history ebook for free as well as discounts and a potential to get more history books for free! Simply visit the link below to join.

Captivatinghistory.com/ebook

Also, make sure to follow us on Facebook, Twitter and Youtube by searching for Captivating History.

Printed in Great Britain
by Amazon

71840403R00061